CHRISTIAN ETHICS

IS VOLUME

58

OF THE

Twentieth Century Encyclopedia of Catholicism

UNDER SECTION

V

THE LIFE OF FAITH

IT IS ALSO THE

113TH

VOLUME IN ORDER OF PUBLICATION

Edited by HENRI DANIEL-ROPS of the Académie Française

CHRISTIAN ETHICS

By DENIS J. B. HAWKINS

HAWTHORN BOOKS · PUBLISHERS · *New York*

First Edition, December, 1963

BJ1249
H39C

NIHIL OBSTAT

Joannes M.T. Barton, S.T.D., L.S.S.

    Censor Deputatus

IMPRIMATUR

✠ Georgius L. Craven

    Episcopus Sebastopolis, Vicarius Generalis

Westmonasterii, die XXV SEPTEMBRIS MCMLXIII

H-9547

CONTENTS

PREFACE

A small book like this can only be selective. I have tried to bring out a few of the main features by which a specifically Christian ethic is distinguished from a purely philosophical morality and to discuss one or two questions of detail on which the Christian attitude might be considered especially susceptible to attack or misunderstanding. Chapter X reproduces, with a slight omission and a slight addition, an article which appeared in the *Clergy Review* for February 1962 under the title of "Arguments in Sexual Ethics". The middle section of Chapter XI, under the heading of "How It Looked in 1937", first appeared under the title of "Militarism and Pacifism" in the number of a long-defunct quarterly called *Arena* for April 1937. I thank the Editor and Proprietors of the *Clergy Review* for permission to use the former article.

D.J.B.H.

CHAPTER I

THE CRISIS OF MORALS

THE NINETEENTH-CENTURY COMPROMISE

The nineteenth century was the great age of the noble
agnostic, and even of the noble atheist. It was generally
assumed that, however much religious belief faded away,
moral principles would remain. If there was to be any change
in moral outlook, it would be in the direction of greater
benevolence and greater disinterestedness. With the cruelties
and superstitions of the past abolished, the moral ideals
hitherto entertained by Christians would only be enhanced in
a new age of free thought and scientific progress.

Even Marx and Engels, though advocating radical changes
in the social and political order, admitted moral progress in
the past and thought of the morality of the Communist para-
dise as completing and fulfilling the moral ideals of mankind.

> That . . . there has on the whole been progress in morality,
> as in all other branches of human knowledge, cannot be
> doubted. But we have not yet passed beyond class morality.
> A really human morality which transcends class antagonisms
> and their legacies in thought becomes possible only at a stage
> of society which has not only overcome class contradictions
> but has even forgotten them in practical life.[1]

As an example of the sort of progress to be expected Engels
offers the disappearance of a precept against theft when

[1] F. Engels: *Anti-Dühring*, Part I, ch. ix, Lawrence and Wishart,
n.d., p. 109.

private property has been abolished: "In a society in which the motive for stealing has been done away with, in which therefore at the very most only lunatics would ever steal, how the teacher of morals would be laughed at who tried solemnly to proclaim the eternal truth: Thou shalt not steal!"[2]

Such a change, if we may suppose it for a moment to be possible, is evidently not a reversal of morality as hitherto understood but the abolition of temptation, while the equality and brotherhood of the ideal Communist society are in the line of ideals already entertained by men. There is no word here of secret police, sanguinary purges, forced labour and concentration camps, although all these things have their possibility implicit in the intermediate phase of the dictatorship of the proletariat, which in practice becomes a permanent dictatorship of the party bosses. But we need not take these unsavoury realities into account when we are considering the intentions of Marx and Engels a hundred years ago.

Certainly, no suspicion crossed the mind of the English nineteenth-century secularist that the general adoption of their views would bring about a moral decline. We may note how Thomas Henry Huxley, in his celebrated Romanes Lecture on *Evolution and Ethics,* assumes the autonomy of moral principles, even though he emphatically acknowledges that they contradict the principles of cosmic evolution.

> The practice of that which is ethically best—what we call goodness or virtue—involves a course of conduct which, in all respects, is opposed to that which leads to success in the cosmic struggle for existence. In place of ruthless self-assertion it demands self-restraint; in place of thrusting aside, or treading down, all competitors, it requires that the individual shall not merely respect, but shall help his fellows; its influence is directed, not so much to the survival of the fittest, as to the fitting of as many as possible to survive.[3]

[2] Loc. cit.
[3] From T. H. Huxley's lecture on "Evolution and Ethics", in T. H. and Julian Huxley: *Evolution and Ethics, 1893–1943,* London, 1947, pp. 81–2.

Yet Huxley had no doubt that moral ideals stood firm in their own right and represented a new stage in the evolution of man which would continue to make progress.

There were some, of course, who, although unwilling or unable to question the general principle of progress, felt vaguely that man was losing something of importance as well as gaining. Note these revealing sentences in a letter of R. L. Nettleship:

> This is one of the things that seem to make modern life so hard—that whilst the voice of all the ages dins into one's ears that we are nearer to God than our fathers, that the world is fuller of divinity than ever, that the truth and goodness and beauty which is our heritage can afford to smile at the heritage of past times, yet this sense of fullness and divineness has to live in an atmosphere from which God seems to have been gradually eliminated, has to find its expression in forms which falsify it. It is as if one said to a man who had been living in the hole of Calcutta, "Now we have got a vacuum, and you may breathe freely."[4]

If a man as reflective as Nettleship found it so difficult to question the inevitability of progress in the moral as in every other order, we need not be surprised at the complacency of the typical Victorian assumption of progress. It took a Newman to see clearly how precarious was the position of absolute moral obligation when deprived of a metaphysical foundation in an Absolute Being. And Newmans were few.

THE CONTEMPORARY SITUATION

Nowadays, as we all know, there is a general complaint among responsible citizens of the lack of moral principle in the population as a whole. Abroad, the present century has seen a degree of cruelty and oppression which our grandfathers would have thought to belong only to a remote and uncivilized past. Even if in our own country we are still com-

---

[4] R. L. Nettleship: *Philosophical Remains*, London, 1901, p. 53.

paratively tolerant; crimes of violence and wanton destructiveness have increased to startling proportions. Sexual licence is followed in practice in a way which corresponds with the tenets of no morality, however free. There are more and more people to whom no moral appeal seems to have any meaning.

What help, meanwhile, is being offered by the professional moralists of the universities? It is not long since moral philosophers thought it their function to explain how we discriminated between right and wrong, and regarded it as within their powers to do so. Either, in the manner of Aristotle, they expounded a form of life which imposed itself on us as appropriate to the nature of man, or at least they held us to possess a sufficient number of general moral intuitions, the categorical imperatives of Kant. Or, perhaps, they combined in their different ways elements from both these approaches.

Nowadays there is scarcely any such positive moral philosophy at the universities. In the recent past the logical positivists told us that what purported to be ethical statements were merely instances of the emotive use of language. When we said that actions were right or wrong, we were really doing no more than utter favourable or unfavourable ejaculations. Down to this day the doyen of British philosophers, Bertrand Russell, confesses that he can give no adequate intellectual justification of the moral attitudes which he recommends. His own attitudes are certainly humane, and it is impossible to withhold respect from a man approaching ninety whose moral convictions are strong enough to make him spend a day sitting on the pavement in order to express them publicly. Yet Russell is the sort of man from whom we might expect a reason as well as a gesture.

Many of our younger contemporary moral philosophers take a similar line. They tell us that, although we can give reasons for particular moral decisions in terms of moral principles, these principles themselves are neither self-evident nor demonstrable. Our basic ethical policy is simply a matter of decision. No doubt these philosophers have themselves adopted moral principles which not only keep them out of the hands of the police but make them, except as philosophers, amiable and worthy members of society. Indeed one cannot help suspecting that these shaky moral philosophies seem acceptable to their authors only because these gentlemen are naturally immune from temptation and strictly predestined to virtue. Yet they are obviously helpless in face of anyone who asks why he should not do this or that if he can do so and get away with it. There is always the danger that their pupils might take them too seriously.

MORALITY AND RELIGION

When secular moralists are so unhelpful it is tempting to follow the example of Miss Elizabeth Anscombe and to propose a thoroughgoing theological theory of morality.[5] According to such a theory the notion of moral obligation presupposes a divine law and becomes meaningless without it. But this would be an excessive reaction. For it is true both that some duties can be recognized without reference to a Creator and that it is significant to ask why a divine law should be obeyed. The ultimate real source of moral obligation resides in the exigencies of the nature of things as eternally perceived by the divine intellect rather than in a fiat of the divine will, and some of these exigencies can be seen by us in their own right. Nevertheless, the acknowledgement of God transforms the field of morality not only by introducing the element of personal allegiance but by putting specific duties in a new light.

We may admit, then, in spite of the disagreement of many contemporary secular moralists, that on a purely secular level we may discover evident duties which follow from our nature and the natures of those with whom we are in relation. Fundamental duties of justice and benevolence need no theological

[5] Cf. G. E. M. Anscombe: "Modern Moral Philosophy," in *Philosophy*, vol. xxxiii, no. 124 (Jan. 1958), pp. 1–19.

reference in order to be recognized. Yet there are other duties which might seem at first sight to belong to the purely human level but which really depend in whole or in part on a recognition of our creaturely status.

For it is not until we perceive ourselves as creatures that we see ourselves as not belonging wholly to ourselves but possessing our lives and powers on trust for the purposes of the Creator. It is because we are not entitled to terminate this trust at will that the religious man, and only the religious man, regards suicide as always wrong. Apart from our relation to God why should we not be sometimes justified in deciding that it was better to depart rather than protract a humanly useless existence? In the same way it makes an immense difference whether we regard our sexual powers as adaptable to our purely human desires or as bestowed on us to use always with a proper respect for the purposes of the Creator. The whole difference between the old Christian and the new secular attitude to sex can be seen to arise from the presence or absence of the sense of creatureliness.

More generally, of course, the acknowledgement of God means that moral obligation is not only a categorical imperative in Kant's meaning but a service for which we are responsible to a personal Lord. We need not, therefore, be surprised that, however far we may be able to develop a moral theory on a purely human basis, the practical difference of moral outlook between the religious and the non-religious man is as great as it has proved itself to be in our own time. In defending a Christian moral theory we are doing a great deal more than merely to assert a few extra obligations owed specifically to God; we are defending a whole dimension of morality which ceases to exist in the absence of religious belief. A purely human moral theory is an academic luxury which has its place in the elaboration of an analytic philosophical understanding of things, but which enjoys a highly precarious existence in the real world.

CHAPTER II

NATURE AND SUPERNATURE

THE FREE GIFT OF GOD

We have seen that, although philosophers can pursue a logical analysis of moral obligation for some distance without reference to religion, morality in the concrete can scarcely maintain itself in purity and fullness without the support of religious belief and practice. But we must take another step forward. The real world in which we live is not merely one in which human reason is led to acknowledge a Creator and to see in its laws the reflection of divine intelligence; it is a world in which the Incarnation has taken place. God has become man in Christ, and "as many as received him, he gave them power to be made the sons of God" (John 1. 12).

We live in a supernatural order of things, an order in which God has revealed himself and communicates himself in grace so that we may reach a final union with him which exceeds our natural powers and their natural fulfilment. Hence any picture which we may be inclined to make of a purely philosophical religion and morality is inadequate to our real situation. Such pictures as have been drawn of a purely natural religion are often, indeed, far from plausible. It is difficult to take very seriously the idea of men assembling to celebrate a philosophical sabbath by chanting the decorous praises of a silent deity. Those vast open spaces to which we are sometimes referred as a suitable religious environment by people who, as called to be members of the Christian community, ought to know better might, however, be enough for natural religion. But all that we can imagine in detail about natural religion is unverifiable hypothesis.

Hence we might begin to wonder whether the existence of man in a purely natural order was a genuine possibility at all. The early Protestant reformers rejected this notion as a figment of the medieval scholastics. Man was of his nature made for communion with God, and without this he was capable of no sort of fulfilment or achievement. Consequently sin and the Fall involved the complete deformation of human nature; sinful man was totally depraved. Within the ancient Church Baius introduced as much of this as he thought compatible with Catholic theology, but the Church judged that he had introduced too much. The Church condemned not only the new doctrines but the ideas of Baius too, and asserted that man can make no natural claim on the kind of communion which God in fact offers to him. This is the gift of God, and it belonged to God's sovereign freedom to bestow it or to withhold it.

Yet such massive tendencies of thought do not easily disappear, and there remain among Catholic theologians such as hold that, although man can make no claim upon the gifts of God, the divine generosity makes it impossible to suppose that God should leave man at a lower level instead of raising him to supernatural union with himself. In our own day Henri de Lubac's striking book called *Surnaturel* has given new life to this direction of thought. Nevertheless, the divine generosity is already manifested in creation, and it seems rash to try to determine exactly how far God's generosity must lead him. We must also acknowledge God's sovereign freedom, not of course between good and evil, but between good and good. It is for God to choose what and how much good he confers upon his creatures.

History, moreover, has not left us without examples of

conceptions of proper human development which seem content to remain on the natural level. Of such pure humanisms the Aristotelian ethic is the most complete and the most familiar example. No doubt, at the end of the *Nicomachean Ethics,* Aristotle exhorts us to live a life as near to that of the gods as possible, but this does not seem to mean more than the life of the philosopher and scientist. For the rest Aristotle's picture of the virtuous man is very much a picture of a fully developed and self-contained humanity. The magnanimous man is quite unlike the saint.

Professor C. D. Broad makes some incisive criticisms of A. E. Taylor's argument in *The Faith of a Moralist* that nothing less than the beatific vision can produce complete human happiness:

> May not our conviction of the comparative worthlessness of the secular life, however much it might be improved in detail, arise from the fact that we view it from outside and are appalled at an endless vista leading to nothing? ... I believe that if *in fact* each man had an unending continuance of much the same kind of life as he now enjoys there would be but few moments in this endless duration at which he would not wish that his life should go on.... Is it quite fair to condemn a certain mode of life, which at most moments has given tolerable satisfaction to most men who are living it, merely because it seems worthless when viewed from a quite exceptional standpoint which a few exceptional people take at a few moments in their lives?... When we assert that to enjoy the beatific vision is man's greatest good, is there not a danger that we may be generalizing from the tastes and capacities of a few very exceptional men to mankind at large?[1]

Broad deserves an honest rejoinder. We must admit that the average Christian is not at all moments actively desiring the beatific vision, and even that the demands of grace involve a certain tension in human life which would be avoided by pure humanism. There are times when, if we are honest with

[1] Prof. C. D. Broad in *Mind* N.S. vol. xl (1931), p. 371.

ourselves, we must recognize that we could willingly sink into the pursuit of an easier ideal. There is also the experience of the attraction of grace, but the facts of human psychology confirm the possibility of a purely natural order and the gratuitous character of the call to a supernatural fulfilment.

SUPERNATURAL LIFE

It is, therefore, through the free divine generosity that we are made capable of a union with God above our natural powers and claims. For a Christian the moral life is caught up into a larger whole, the life of religion in response to that divine invitation. The Christian life, as the means to a super-natural end, is itself supernatural, depending upon the grace of God bestowed upon us. This is that more abundant life of which the Gospel speaks, neither abolishing our natural tendencies with their appropriate fulfilment nor simply added on to them as something wholly apart from them but permeat-ing our natural life and giving supernatural significance to our natural activity while at the same time going beyond the possibilities of nature left to itself.

Since the Gospel speaks of this in terms of a permanent life, its theological analysis has to be in terms not only of transient conscious acts but of habitual dispositions implanted in the soul. Such dispositions are discernible only in their effects, for in themselves they are below the level of consciousness. The general effect of recent psychology of the unconscious has been, whether fairly or not, to persuade men that below the conscious threshold they harbour a shaming conglomera-tion of disreputable tendencies. It is just as well to remember that our good dispositions, the virtues, are equally in them-selves below the threshold, and it is still more reassuring to know that it is at that level that God is working in us to pro-duce and foster the supernatural life.

The intrinsically supernatural virtues, the theological vir-tues, are summed up in the Pauline triad of faith, hope and

charity. By faith we are enabled in some measure to think on
the divine level, not merely accepting God's revelation of
himself but finding an ever fuller meaning in it. By hope we
direct our lives towards their supernatural fulfilment in union
with God, trusting in divine help to bring us to it through all
difficulties and troubles. By charity we are able to love God
with the love of a friend and a son by adoption, a love which
corresponds in some degree with God's gift of himself. By
possessing the habitual dispositions of faith, hope and charity,
implanted in us or infused into us by God, we have a permanent supernatural life and are in a state of grace with God.

The momentous consequence of all this is that men must,
in reality, live either above or below the purely human level.
The modern world provides us with enough examples of what
happens when men live in disregard of the call of grace.
Modern man is surprised when he aims at a pure humanism
and finds that the result is moral disintegration and sheer
inhumanity. He need not be surprised. If he turns away from
God's supernatural invitation, he cannot expect to maintain
himself at the full height of enlightened reason and purely
human benevolence. If he is not seeking to realize the angel
in him, the beast in him inevitably tends to take charge.

It is equally true, however, that we cannot lead a supernatural life if we neglect the basic human virtues. Nature is
the foundation upon which the structure of grace is built, and
the building cannot be broader or firmer than the foundation.
A debased supernaturalism, which despises the natural world
and man's natural development, is as harmful in its way as a
mere humanism. There are far too many Catholics who seem
in practice to think that, apart from sexual sins, the only real
sins are missing Mass on Sunday and eating meat on Friday.
The narrowness of their minds and their lack of charity and
kindness towards others do not worry them in the least. The
same sort of defect can be observed in a narrow ecclesiasti-
cism, an incense-laden atmosphere of living to which no fresh
air penetrates from the wider world and nothing seems to

matter except the affairs of the Church conceived in a purely institutional sense.

These two introductory chapters have sketched the basic ideas involved in Christian living. We do not intend to draw out at length the more obvious consequences of these principles. Our purpose is to consider mainly some of the problems which suggest themselves and the puzzles which may disturb us when we reflect on this scheme of things.

CHAPTER III

DUTY AND

SELF-FULFILMENT

THE PROBLEM

So far we have tried to show in a fairly conventional way how religion, and specifically the Christian faith, enlarges and reinforces a purely human morality, but we may at this point be struck by a very serious misgiving. This is no less than the fear that the introduction of religion nevertheless compromises the very centre of ethics. For the essence of duty is that it presents itself as something to be done whatever the consequences may be. If there is a just God, however, he must be believed to reward the virtuous and to punish the vicious. In that case the doing of one's duty seems to be reduced to a matter of enlightened self-interest. Morality is vulgarized by being brought down to the merely prudential level.

We cannot evade this difficulty by tampering with the unconditional character of moral duty. Whatever we may think of Kant's theory of knowledge, and however uncongenial we may find that eminent philosopher's style, we must admit that he rings true when he proclaims the categorical imperative of morality. All other imperatives are at least implicitly conditional. If you want to catch the next train for London, you must leave the house now. But you may not want to catch the next train, and in this case the *must* evaporates. Even if you necessarily desire an end, as everyone must desire in some sense to be happy, a means to this end is still a means, and its imperative character is conditioned by the end to which it conduces. But a moral duty is affected by no end beyond itself. We ought to fulfil it at any cost, for no end, however attractive, can justify morally evil means.

Among more recent thinkers we may remember H. A. Prichard, whose whole work in ethics, from the article on *Does Moral Philosophy Rest on a Mistake?* to the inaugural lecture on *Duty and Interest*, is a continuous polemic against any attempt to find a justification for duty, or even to fill out the idea of duty with any other consideration whatever. The function of the moral philosopher begins and ends with pointing out that, when we recognize a duty, there is nothing more to be said; we have simply to set ourselves to fulfil it. All the great moralists, from Plato to Butler, and even to Kant when he gets beyond the bare fact of the categorical imperative, are rebuked by Prichard for compromising in one way or another the purity of the ideal of duty for duty's sake. One cannot help imagining Prichard at the gate of heaven, firmly refusing admission to a reward which would mar the disinterestedness of right action.

Although a suspicion of something overstrained in Prichard's ideal already thus suggests itself, the uneasiness remains about a religious conception of life in which the attainment of heaven and the avoidance of hell are given an exclusive prominence. That religion has sometimes been presented in repellently commercial terms cannot be denied. The attitude lightly represented by the lines

> It is clearly laid down by the Council of Trent
> That the rate of repayment's ten thousand per cent

has sometimes been expressed and understood more seriously. The difficulty is whether, if divine rewards and punishments are real, such an attitude can be avoided.

REFLECTIONS ON THE HUMAN LEVEL

Perhaps we have been making too sharp an antithesis between the ethics of duty and the ethics of self-fulfilment. It is noteworthy that few moral philosophies exist which do not manage to make room for both factors in varying proportions, and we must not assume too easily that they are all internally inconsistent. While the nearest thing to the Kantian categorical imperative in ancient philosophy is to be found in Stoicism, with its list of appropriate values which one was simply morally bound to promote, this stern sense of duty has a setting in a quest for independence and self-sufficiency which will bring peace of mind to the Stoic sage even if positive happiness is denied him.

Prichard takes Plato to task for thinking it desirable to show that the virtuous man will be happy, but it is clear at least that Plato does not think of the good life exclusively in this light. Although the vision of intelligible beauty and ideal good are the highest self-fulfilment, the philosopher returns to help his less privileged fellow-men not because this will add to his happiness but simply because it becomes him to do so. That Prichard was mistaken in holding that the good for Plato always meant a personal good is evident when we think of the insistence of the Platonic Socrates that it is better to suffer evil than to do it. Since the evil which we must not do is an objective evil, the good which we ought to do is an objective good.

There is, of course, much more ground for regarding Aristotle's ethic as a search for self-fulfilment. The *eudaimonia* which is our supreme end is essentially happiness, and the most prominent feature of Aristotle's discussion is to describe the means of attaining it. Nevertheless, the principle known in a more recent language as *noblesse oblige*, the principle that what is noble or absolutely good should be done for its own sake even when it conflicts with what is expedient or pleasant for ourselves, recurs often enough in Aristotle to show that he did not conceive the moral life entirely in egoistic terms.

In modern philosophy, similarly, few have been as imperceptive as Hobbes in interpreting morality as a higher egoism. Although the Utilitarians professed to derive moral principles from selfish desires, they always tacitly presupposed that a combination of reasonable egoisms would result in an objective harmony, and, when we reach John Stuart Mill, the obligation to promote the happiness of others appears with full explicitness if not with any great effort to maintain its consistency with original egoism. In short, the history of ethics seems to show that, however strong an egoistic element may appear in this system or that, it is scarcely ever without some counterweight of the nature of objective duty. It seems hazardous to suppose, with Prichard, that these elements are necessarily in opposition to each other.

If we take the factor of objective and unconditional duty as ethically fundamental, we must nevertheless admit that our own good is one of the goods which we have to take into account in arriving at a judgement about what is our duty. Moreover, it is abundantly evident that our activity is more constantly concerned with our own good than with that of anyone else. It is also true that the doing of our duty is always a form of moral self-fulfilment even when it does not promote our good in any other way. Although the frequent repetition of "What a good boy am I", as in the nursery rhyme, is to be deprecated, it must be a source of humble satisfaction to be able to look back and find that we have succeeded in avoiding the line of least resistance and doing our duty in a case of difficulty.

Besides, can we refrain from asking, like Kant himself in spite of his devotion to the categorical imperative, whether right action could be absolutely imperative in an immoral universe? The extent to which each of us can change the world is so small that, unless we could think of our moral striving as a co-operation with a cosmic moral force which would eventually be manifested in the accomplishment of perfect justice, we might well be tempted to despair and to dismiss our personal efforts towards righteousness as futile. Kant no doubt exaggerated the validity of this line of thought. If it were peremptory, the moral imperative would no longer be absolutely categorical. The recognition of duty must in the last resort be independent of a judgement about the ultimate success of our efforts. Nevertheless, the psychological strength of the sense of duty would be considerably lessened if we suspected that the universe was in effect laughing at our relative impotence.

Finally, obligation is not the whole of the moral life. Not only are there greater goods which are not strictly of obligation, but there is a greater good in the sphere of motive than the bare sense of duty. Love preserves the substance of duty while transcending its limitations of sympathy. In particular, perfect love would abolish our present problem because it would make the distinction between self and other irrelevant. This thought gains its full power on the religious level, to which we are about to transfer our attention, but it is already indicated by human ethical reflection as that state beyond mere morality to which morality itself points.

THE ANSWER ON THE RELIGIOUS LEVEL

There can be no doubt for the Christian that fidelity to duty and self-fulfilment will eventually coincide in accordance with absolute divine justice. Eternity will rectify the inequalities of time. God will reward the good and punish the wicked. It remains true, however, that the motive of right action is precisely its rightness and not the advantage which it will entail on the other side of the grave. Not that it is wrong for the religious man to desire heaven any more than it is wrong for the secular moralist to desire whatever good he may anticipate. Very much to the contrary, but this is not the spring of dutiful action precisely as such. Duty is to be done because it is seen to be objectively due.

Much less than the secular moralist, however, will the religious man want to linger in the bare thought of duty. If all morality points in the end beyond itself to love, religious morality points in this direction more clearly and more urgently. What is distinctive of the moral teaching of the gospels is not a new code of morality or a new theory of its basis, but the insistence on raising morality to the level of love. The commandments are to find their full meaning and completion in the love of God and of our neighbour for God's sake.

There may, of course, be a possessive as well as a disinterested kind of love. The former need not in general be called a selfish love, for that would sound as if it were never legitimate. The love that men have for mere things must always be in some sense possessive. And it is obviously right and natural that we should find our own satisfaction in relationship with our friends and families, but such a possessive love is never enough when another person is concerned. Persons demand and deserve to be loved for their own sake, so that their good becomes our good and it is our joy to benefit them. If a man loved his friends and family only for the pleasure they gave him, he would not properly be said to love them at all.

An insensitive eighteenth-century theologian, Bolgeni († 1811), maintained that all love was in the last resort egoistic, so that we could not have a disinterested love of God. But Christ taught that the greatest love was to give oneself for one's friends, and he told us to pray that God's name might be hallowed, his kingdom come and his will be done before we mentioned our own needs. He said to his apostles: "If you loved me, you would indeed be glad because I go to the Father" (John 14. 28), in spite of their thus losing his visible presence. There is no doubt, then, that since we are called to be the friends and sons of God, we are to have for God a real love

of friendship (*amor amicitiae*) and not merely a love of desire
(*amor concupiscentiae*).

Fénelon's mistake, therefore, was not that he magnified
the disinterested love of God but that he preached the desira-
bility of a state in which our desire of union with God would
be entirely transcended by the pure love of God for his own
sake. It is also right and necessary that we should desire to
possess God in the beatific vision. In the end there may and
should be perfect harmony between our love of God for
himself and our love of him as bestowing himself upon us.
But those theologians seem to be reasonable who assign the
possessive love of God to hope rather than charity among the
Pauline triad. For, if hope is restricted to the confidence which
we have in God's help to us in reaching him, it presupposes
the desire of God, and we should have logically to speak of
faith, charity and hope rather than of faith, hope and charity.

We now see what it means to say that we cannot save
our souls without charity. It means that the mere desire of
God for our own sake is not enough to lead to the fulfilment
of that desire. It is only in so far as we have some spark of
the love of God for God's sake that we shall attain to union
with him. On that level our problem disappears. It is right
that we should desire God, and our right actions lead certainly
to the fulfilment of that desire, but our actions are only
fully right when they include also the love of God for what he
is in himself.

In this light we understand the structure of St Thomas
Aquinas's synthesis of the Christian life in the *Prima* and
Secunda Secundae. As usual St Thomas keeps as near to Aristotle as possible. Hence the general question is how man can
reach complete happiness, blessedness or *eudaimonia*, but
this is now identified with the possession of God in the
beatific vision. Right action, in which man co-operates with
divine grace, is seen as the means to attain this final end. But
that St Thomas recognizes that the proper character of moral
obligation is due to the absolute and objective goodness of

what it prescribes becomes clear, for example, when he discusses the due relationship of the human to the divine will.

> In order that man's will should be good, it must be in conformity with God's will . . . Whatever God wills, he wills under the aspect of common good, which is his own goodness, the good of the whole universe . . . Whence, in order that anyone should rightly will some particular good, it is necessary that, while this particular good is materially the object of will, what is formally willed should be the common and divine good.[1]

St Thomas's teaching about charity completes the same line of thought.

> Faith and hope make contact with God in so far as he bestows on us the knowledge of truth or the power of attaining good; but charity makes contact with God in himself and rests in him rather than in anything he bestows upon us. Hence charity excels faith and hope and, consequently, every other virtue also.[2]

[1] St Thomas Aquinas: *Summa Theologica*, Ia–IIae, qu. 19, art. 9–10.
[2] Op. cit., IIa–IIae, qu. 23, art. 6.

CHAPTER IV

CHRISTIAN HUMANISM

RELIGION AND THE WORLD

Although the lives of the saints, as they used to be conventionally written, may not tell us much about what the saints really were and did, they tell us a good deal about what people have supposed saints to be. When we read that the holy man observed a fast on Fridays even when he was an infant at the breast, that he grew up to insist on wearing the roughest of hair shirts and sleeping on a bed of sharp spikes, and that he never took the slightest interest in the good of society, the advance of knowledge, or the beauties of nature and art, we may have a well-founded suspicion and a justifiable hope that this is complete nonsense, but we are bound to take seriously the mentality of those who concocted it or who accepted it as true and admirable. There is no doubt that many people have supposed that saints were really like this and that, the more extreme their rejection of the world was, the more clearly their holiness was evident.

That there is an ascetic element in religion, and indeed in ordinary morality, no one will wish to deny. But it seems so clear in theoretical abstraction that this is a negative element which is valid only as subordinate to, as a necessary condition of, a positive development. The Greek ideal of a harmonious development of the whole man is enlarged and not abolished by the clearer Christian conception of man's orientation to God. For God is the creator of the whole world, and it is no honour to God to despise what he has created.

It would be different if there were two gods, a good god who created spirit and an evil god who created matter. Then we could do homage to one by turning our backs on the work of the other. But Christians are no Manichees, and theoretically at least we acknowledge the Jewish and Christian God who saw what he had created and all was good.

Not only, however, has hagiography often been cultivated by unwitting Manichees, but we far too frequently find that the ordinary believer displays the narrow-mindedness without the sanctity. It all seems the negation of that more abundant life promised us by Christ. Yet we need to reassure ourselves that the ideal of a wide Christian humanism is not flying in the face of Christian history. What does Christian history really tell us about it?

THE BEGINNINGS OF CHRISTIAN HUMANISM

The conditions under which the Christian Church worked during the first three centuries at once suggest a practical limitation to the ideal of Christian humanism. For frequent persecutions and constant liability to persecution do not constitute a congenial environment for the uninterrupted development of the things of the mind. Yet it is striking to note how much intellectual development went on within the Christian Church even in the early era of persecution.

Already in the New Testament, at any rate in St Paul and St John, a theological comment accompanies the report of the teaching of Christ. St Paul, of course, is always anxious to disclaim any dependence on purely human wisdom and to admit that his gospel will be foolishness to the man unenlightened by divine grace. Yet, with all respect to St Paul and without derogating from the inspired character of his writings, it may be thought that he sometimes protests too much. Was it not perhaps a certain consciousness of superior intellect and education that made him so intent on declaring that he was in the same position as all the rest in relation to

God's message? And might not this unconcealable superiority have been the ground of some of the opposition which he makes clear that he encountered? We can well imagine some of the first Christians becoming impatient with this subtle and difficult new teacher when they compared him with the comparative simplicities of the other apostles. At any rate, if we can hardly claim St Paul as a Christian humanist, he was certainly one who brought very considerable intellectual resources to bear on his way of presenting the Christian faith.

In the Fourth Gospel a first step is taken in the long history of the Christian use of Greek thought. The Greeks had constantly spoken of a cosmic Logos or Word, and, since Antiochus of Ascalon had brought about a certain fusion between the Platonic and the Stoic traditions, the term could appear in the context of almost any school of thought. Hence it is useless to ask from what particular author the term is borrowed for the purposes of the Gospel. The Gospel nowhere puts it into the mouth of Christ himself; it is evidently an illustration chosen by the evangelist to enable a Greek audience to make an approach to understanding the relationship of Christ in his pre-existent divinity to his Father. As Augustine was to say long afterwards, Greek philosophy had already taught in a way that in the beginning was the Word, and the Word was with God; the new Gospel proclamation was that the Word had become flesh and dwelt among us.

Thus Greek thought began to acquire a positive significance in the context of Christianity, and St Justin in the second century could speak without embarrassment of those among the ancient Greeks as well as among the Hebrews who had in their measure been enlightened by the Logos before his incarnation in Christ. The Alexandrian Fathers, Clement and Origen, follow in the same path in acknowledging the way in which Greek philosophy prepared the way for Christ and in using its resources freely in the interpretation of the faith. Too freely, it may indeed be objected, but only a carping critic would want to blame Clement and Origen for not getting all the proportions right at once.

The main stream of Christian tradition seems, therefore, to have been open from the beginning to the values of its human environment, and this openness is naturally only increased when Christianity ceases to be persecuted and becomes the official religion of the Roman Empire. Not only is there a natural use of Greek, and especially Platonic, philosophical ideas in the formulation of Christian theology but a literary education continued to be based on the same classical authors as before. There is even a certain last flowering of Latin poetry among Christian writers like Prudentius and Paulinus, Ausonius, Sedulius and Sidonius Apollinaris. If these are not names of the first rank, they make a special appeal in their pursuit of a humane Muse in an age when classical civilization was visibly becoming more fragile and tottering to its collapse.

The other side, the kind of religion which turns altogether away from the world, is seen in the hermits and monks of the Egyptian desert. Even they, of course, may be viewed as the Christian descendants of the Cynic sages of the later classical world, but neither the Cynics nor the Fathers of the Desert were humanists. The lives of the Desert Fathers have been so embroidered in legend that it is not easy to guess how they really lived, but they certainly must have been exponents of the simple life and of concentration on the one thing necessary to a degree which we scarcely relish imagining.

In the West St Benedict organized a much more moderate kind of monasticism, but it was Cassiodorus who widened the scope of the Western monasteries to become preservers of part at least of the ancient classical culture. At the same period, in the sixth century, when the Western empire had come to an end and men accepted a decline of civilization as naturally as the men of the nineteenth century expected progress, Boethius, himself to be the victim of a barbarian king, was imperturbably making his plans to latinize Plato and Aristotle while also applying a systematic logic to theological questions in a manner which looks forward to the medieval schoolmen. That his consolation in his imprisonment was of a philosophical order has disturbed some myopic critics who fail to notice that he made an eminently Christian selection from his sources and need not have thought himself any the less a Christian for acknowledging freely all that he owed to Greek thought. In this way he set an example of Christian humanism which continued to shine out fitfully even in the darkest of the dark ages.

LATER CHRISTIAN HUMANISM

It was natural to look at the Christian attitude to classical culture from the point of view of humanism in a restricted sense, for this culture came into existence independently of Christianity, and the Christian attitude towards it could be most readily seen in relation to its thought and literature. But medieval civilization was largely a creation of the Church. The great bishops and abbots of the Dark Ages had been the last repositories of Roman order. The germs of civilization had been kept alive by the Church in the Dark Ages. When they budded again, they might be expected to reveal what had happened to them when made the instruments of a Christian purpose.

The Middle Ages are evidently a highly theologically-minded period. No period even of genuinely Christian civilization is likely to be quite so dominated by theology again, for civilization is hardly likely to be ever again so much in the hands of churchmen. Must we say on that account that it was not humanistic? On the contrary, for the best medieval theology was open-minded enough to find room for, while applying to its own purposes, all the secular and scientific knowledge that was currently available.

This state of mind was not, of course, reached without opposition. We remember how, in the eleventh century, St Peter Damian was already suspicious of those monastic grammarians who might be accused of laying more store by the rules of Donatus than by the rule of St Benedict. Yet, if Peter Damian is the author of the hymn *Ad perennis vitae fontem,* he was no bad poet himself. St Bernard opposed not only some of the conclusions of Abelard, in which he was no doubt justified, but also the whole new spirit of rational inquiry which was typified at the beginning of the twelfth century by that ill-fated thinker. Gilbert de la Porrée had to stand up to Bernard too, and, as a highly respected bishop, was able to do so with more success. For it was certainly the spirit of Abelard which triumphed in the course of the twelfth century.

For the best in the thought of the thirteenth century we look to St Thomas Aquinas, and what is impressive about St Thomas in this matter is that he does not find it necessary to argue in favour of a wide-minded synthesis; he thinks it enough to present it. In the *Prima Secundae* he incorporates the Aristotelian ethical ideal into a view of the Christian life without, at least, betraying any of the misgivings which even a modern theologian might feel in wondering whether it could be thus incorporated without remainder. The thirteenth-century theologian was also a philosopher, and the philosopher might be a naturalist as well, like Albertus Magnus, or a speculative physicist, like Grosseteste.

Hence it is a mistake to reserve the name of humanism for the more literary revival of the classics at the Renaissance. Nor, on the other hand, is Renaissance humanism to be unduly denigrated in its relation to Christianity. There is a genuine charm in the Platonism of Marsilius Ficinus and Pico della Mirandola in fifteenth-century Florence, while at the same period Christian humanism reached its highest expression in painting with Botticelli and Piero della Francesca. No doubt Renaissance humanism had its all too human side, which attracted the condemnation of both the Reformation and the Counter-Reformation, but what Christian humanism might have become is evident in men like Erasmus and More, Contarini, Pole and Sadoleto.

Nevertheless, the later Middle Ages had also seen the opening of a breach between practical piety and not only philosophy but even theology. The most striking example is that curiously lopsided masterpiece, the *Imitation of Christ*. As Thomas à Kempis drives his edifying bulldozer over the more intellectual elements in religion, he seems sublimely unconscious of the possibility of retort. "What is the use of arguing high things about the Trinity if you lack humility and so displease the Trinity?" (I i 7). Of course, but what is more likely to inspire a true creaturely humility than to reflect on the mystery of the Trinity? "I would rather feel compunction than know its definition" (I i 9). Obviously, but surely it is easier to feel compunction if you know what it is that you are asked to feel. "Why should we bother about genera and species?" (I iii 6). Because that is the way in which human minds work when they try to understand God's world a little.

And so one could continue. No doubt there was a lot of dry-as-dust theology in Thomas à Kempis's time, and this helps to explain his outburst, but the remedy is perhaps worse than the disease if it consists in a *devotio moderna* which is indifferent to theology. Yet this tendency towards an undoctrinal, and therefore sentimental, piety established itself in the traditions both of the Reformation and of the Counter-Reformation and is still a feature of popular religion. It has doubtless contributed a great deal to the decline of an ideal of Christian humanism.

On a wider background this is a symptom of a division between the sacred and the secular in which religion was increasingly forced on to the defensive by the progressive advances and the exclusive claims of the secular. Instead of finding in religion the integrating principle of a complete human outlook the religious man has fallen back on preserving a corner of his mind unaffected by the secular because unrelated to it. This kind of religion is marked by a spiritual infantilism, because it is really the result of defending a part of an infantile outlook untouched by later influences. Hence people tend to show a preference for childish prayers and jingly hymn-tunes, and they want paintings and statues which are like nothing more than the dolls that surrounded them in the nursery. They are afraid to seek religious maturity, for they have a deep-seated uneasiness that any degree of religious maturity would tend to corrupt the purity of their faith. Faith is no longer the victory that overcomes the world but an uneasy refuge from what could only too easily be acknowledged as a more real world. In this way the question of Christian humanism is very relevant to our present needs.

ELEMENTS OF A SOLUTION

There can be no doubt about the answer to the question in principle. The worth of everything is from God, and nothing which has any value can have its worth destroyed or diminished by the special action of that same God in history. The Christian ethical ideal cannot be less of a whole man than the Greek ideal; rather it adds a new dimension and a fuller wholeness.

That this wholeness is not to be reached without cost is, of course, obvious too. Already from Aristotle's point of view the maximum development of the whole man involves for each constituent an optimum development which is not a maximum. The harmonious integration of the whole calls for temperance or moderation in relation to the parts. This continues to be a fundamental psychological and ethical principle.

From the Christian point of view there is nothing which might not in particular circumstances have to be sacrificed to the one thing necessary. The primary foundation of Christian asceticism is the need to be ready to surrender anything whatever which may turn out to be incompatible with the service of God. At a period which has produced Belsen, Auschwitz

and the labour camps of Siberia we can scarcely feel spiritu-
ally secure if we let ourselves become too dependent on the
amenities of civilization, however good these may be in their
way. The only safe maxim is to limit our desires, even for
what is in itself perfectly legitimate.

Here we must make a distinction between what are primarily enjoyments, even if in themselves perfectly harmless,
and the great positive secular values. About the former we
may well on second thoughts wonder whether what we are
tempted to dismiss as the enthusiastic exaggerations of the
saints are really so far from the mark. In some cases we shall
be justified in thinking that a holy person's judgement was
at fault, and we must always uphold the principle that God,
in creating a world which is in so many ways enjoyable, did
not want us to be indifferent to it. Nevertheless, it is abomin-
ably easy to become absorbed in, and dependent on, creature-
comforts, and we may conjecture the length of our necessary
future purgatory from what will be required to wean us from
our deep-seated attachment to things of a sort no longer available after death. Asceticism is only a means, and there is a
just limit to all means, but we should acknowledge that we
are strongly tempted to draw the limit too soon.

With what may be called the great secular values the case
is different. Their actual prosecution may have to be subordinated, or even completely sacrificed, to the direct service
of God at particular times and in particular cases, but this
is a special need to be made out. In general we can say without hesitation that whatever contributes to making a complete
man contributes also to making a complete Christian. The
Christian is all the better a Christian for being also an active
citizen and taking an interest in the progress of knowledge
and the products of letters and the arts. So the saint is all
the more a saint if he succeeds in being a saint while retaining
wide human interests as well. From the later Middle Ages
onwards the secular has tended to detach itself somewhat
harshly from the sacred. We cannot go back to the exclusive

theological predominance of earlier medieval civilization. But the remedy is not for religion to retire into a sheltered corner and to leave the world alone. The remedy is to recover the sacredness of the secular, the value which belongs to everything in a world created by God, and to reassert the full development of the genuinely human as a Christian as well as a Greek ideal.

CHAPTER V

CONTEMPLATION AND ACTION

GREEK IDEAS OF CONTEMPLATION

We are all familiar with the use made by writers on the Christian life of the distinction between contemplation and action, and the superiority attributed to the former. In a sense, of course, this principle is obvious, for action is necessarily for the sake of something beyond it and, if we ask what is beyond it in the life of the soul, this is a state of being, experience or, in a wide sense, contemplation. Hence action belongs to the realm of means and contemplation possesses more of the nature of an end. Yet the word *contemplation* has been used in such a bewildering variety of meanings that not all the applications of this principle are beyond question. The principle of the superiority of contemplation to action has sometimes been used with an unduly narrowing effect on the conception of the Christian life.

If we want to disentangle some of the ways in which people have spoken of contemplation, we must go back to the fundamental sense in which contemplation is a translation of the Greek word *theoria.* It will be remembered that Aristotle in the *Nicomachean Ethics,* after having considered the various virtues or habits of right action, asks at the end wherein the highest form of human life consists and answers that this is in the theoretical or contemplative life. By this he means the life of philosophical and scientific research. Although he says that this resembles the life of the gods, there is nothing specifically religious about this conception. He means simply that, if we cannot be personally immortal, and he did not think that we were, we could at any rate devote our passing life to the consideration of fundamental and unchanging truths.

The theoretical life as envisaged by Aristotle presupposes an adequate income, though not necessarily great wealth, and a sufficient number of slaves to attend to practical needs and to leave the master free for his intellectual pursuits. It is the life of a cultivated Athenian gentleman. Evidently it can be the privilege only of a few. In this equalitarian age it is likely to incur considerable disapproval, but one may be permitted to find a certain charm in Aristotle's unselfconscious *snobisme*. Certainly his ideal form of human life would be a very pleasant one.

But what on earth, the less erudite reader will be asking, has this to do with what Christians have understood by the contemplative life? We must go back from Aristotle to his master Plato, who also preached an ideal of contemplation. The philosopher found his fulfilment in the contemplation of the eternal and unchanging Forms which were the models to which the changing things of the world of space and time deficiently approximated. In the *Symposium* Plato describes how we can rise from an appreciation of beautiful things to a view of the ideal essence of Beauty. In the *Republic* he tells us that only the philosopher has a clear view of the Form of the Good, the value of all values, while other men live in a world of shadows and reflections. The philosopher has to descend again into the shadow-world in order to assist his fellows, but it is clear that the supreme human experience is the contemplation of the Forms, and especially of the Form of the Good.

This comes nearer to a religious conception of the purpose of human life, although it is not altogether religious, since the Forms are not gods. They are essentially eternal *objects*, to be contemplated, even if more perfectly, by the gods as by us. If there is one supreme creative god, the Demiurge of the *Timaeus*, he is not to be identified with the Form of the Good or with any other form. In shaping the world he, like all other intellects, must contemplate forms outside himself.

A fully religious conception of the place of contemplation in human life is characteristic of Plotinus and the Neoplatonists. For Plotinus the supreme intellect, the Nous, contains the Forms in systematic unity. The supreme being, the One, is suprapersonal, transcending the multiplicity of understanding and of the Forms themselves. In rising through the contemplation of the Nous to unity with the One the human mind passes beyond the intellectual life to a mystical rapture which can no longer be analysed and described. When speaking of the ascent of the soul to mystical union Plotinus distinguishes the preparatory stages of purgation and illumination in terms which have perpetuated themselves in the theory of Christian mysticism.

CHRISTIAN IDEAS OF CONTEMPLATION

Plotinus, of course, belongs to the third century A.D., so that he is later than Clement of Alexandria and was a junior contemporary of Origen. Specifically Plotinian ideas owe their place in the theory of Christian mysticism largely to the influence of the works of the Pseudo-Dionysius, long thought to have been the genuine Dionysius the Areopagite converted by St Paul. Nevertheless, the Neoplatonic modification of Platonism had been to a considerable extent anticipated by the Middle Academy beginning with Antiochus of Ascalon a century before Christ. Middle Platonism was a pervasive element in an intellectual atmosphere which was sufficiently akin to Christianity to begin to influence it as soon as it came into contact with the Greek world. It is to this general atmosphere of thought rather than to any particular thinker that we must attribute the way in which, for example, the Fourth Gospel makes use of the notion of the Logos to illustrate the relationship of the Son to the Father in the Trinity. St Paul himself was enough of a Hellenist to single out the direct vision of God as the primary feature in the state which we call Heaven.

The Alexandrian Fathers, Clement and Origen, inaugurating the systematic study of theology, recognized that they were in the line of Greek ideas of the values of human life. Like Aristotle they pointed to the value of systematic thinking, but for them as Christians the highest kind of systematic thinking was theology, the reflective elaboration of what we could say about God both from his creation and from what he had revealed of himself in history. Through theological meditation the Christian could attain to a genuine *gnosis,* not the occult farrago of the Gnostics but a progressively profounder understanding and realization of divine truth.

It did not occur to these good men to separate theology from prayer, to look on theology as some sort of arid conceptual analysis while the only real knowledge of God was to be obtained in some totally different way. Why indeed should such nonsense have occurred to them? For what motive can there be for any persistent theological thinking but the love of God? And to what result can it tend but an increase in the love of God? The theology of the Fathers continues to be a "kneeling theology", a theology which finds its fulfilment in prayer and in supernatural union with God.

The same is true of the Middle Ages at least up to and including St Thomas Aquinas. No doubt the new and more explicitly logico-analytic methods of theological inquiry had aroused the suspicions of conservatives like St Bernard, who preferred to maintain a more biblical and patristic line. But, if the new Scholastic theology vindicated itself in the end, it was precisely because and in so far as it showed itself to be equally capable of ministering to the needs of the spirit. Much has sometimes been made of the declaration of St

Thomas when he felt his end approaching, that what he had written seemed to him like straw in comparison with what had been shown to him, but this is no more than the natural and inevitable reaction of anyone who tries to write on any great subject and compares the result with what he would have liked it to be. The artist has the same feeling when he looks at his finished painting and compares it with what he wanted to express. Such a recognition of imperfection is certainly no condemnation of the achievement of the *Summa Theologica*.

It must be admitted, however, that the life went out of the theology of the fourteenth and fifteenth centuries. Apart from the logic-chopping of the theologians the anti-theological bias of the *Imitation of Christ* would be inexplicable. It is from the later Middle Ages that we must date the breach between a comparatively lifeless theology and an untheological spirituality which still plagues us. The Benedictine tradition of a harmony of study and prayer was too deeply rooted in history to be altogether overwhelmed; the Dominicans, in so far as they were faithful to St Thomas, retained a sound exemplar; the Franciscans had a model of "kneeling theology" in St Bonaventure. But newer movements in the Church tended to dissociate theological thinking from spiritual development, and we all know how far modern popular piety can be from the doctrines which are its proper foundation.

Here, then, is a separation which ought never to have come about. If we think of theological reflection as the Christian equivalent of Aristotelian *theoria* and of contemplative prayer as the Christian equivalent of Platonic *theoria*, we should see them as two sides of the same thing. No doubt we should also accept an ascending scale from stages in which analytic thinking is a predominant element to stages in which it has done the major part of its work and a massive realization of divine truth is in place, and we must leave room beyond this for the special divine favours received by the mystic. Nor, evidently, does every Christian begin the life of prayer by theological meditation in an academic sense. But he does begin by an assimilation of doctrine. Hence we must not separate theological thinking from the ordinary Christian's reflection on his faith, nor must we make a discontinuity between the prayer of the ordinary Christian, theologian or not, and the prayer of the saint. Even the humblest forms of Christian reflection and prayer depend on the infused habit of faith, and even the most sublime instances of infused mystical knowledge are received and appreciated by the natural intellect.

In practice, however, we must acknowledge that the ordinary modern Christian sees little affinity between theological reflection and contemplative prayer. Since these both correspond with aspects of the meaning of the Greek word *theoria,* we may say that there has been a split in the meaning of contemplation. Moreover, the retreat from the intellect in spirituality has had some rather odder results. It has become conventional to insist that the fruit of prayer is the production of "affections". If this is simply taken to mean that all genuine prayer leads to and increases the love of God, it is, of course, perfectly true. Yet it sounds far too often as if spiritual writers are recommending some psychologically quite impossible state of affairs in which the thought of God gives place to the love of God. One's heart bleeds for any good nun who supposes that she is intended to spend a considerable amount of time early in the morning, on an empty stomach, trying to reach some almost objectless state of emotion.

The point is that we cannot divide thought and will in this way. Our feelings and volitions are the psychological colouring of experiences and thoughts. Awareness and conation are two sides of one and the same concrete reality which is human experience. So far from conflicting, these two sides stimulate and enhance one another. Hence, if we must allude to a third alleged meaning of religious contemplation, in which it is the complete opposite of *theoria* as being a purely emotional state, we must add that it is not only a religious but a psychological monstrosity.

Another complication arises when we speak of the contemplative and active lives as expressing the ideals of different types of religious order. Here, of course, it is a question of their predominant, not of their sole, function. The contemplative is not exempt from all outward activity, nor is the active religious intended to spend the day in an uninterrupted round of feverish activity. But what exactly is meant by the contemplation of the contemplative? No doubt the monastic peace is a favourable environment both for the cultivation of theological study and the development of the higher states of prayer, but there is no order which confines its membership to theological luminaries or even to budding mystics. The essential feature of the contemplative life as the form of life of a whole community is rather the predominant place assigned to the praise of God in the Divine Office. We may, then, speak of a third legitimate meaning of contemplation when we describe the life of the praise of God as the contemplative life.

THE RELATION OF CONTEMPLATION AND ACTION

When we bring together these various meanings of contemplation, and when we compare them with action, it is evident that there should ideally be no conflict. No doubt thought has more of the nature of an end and action of a means, but that does not imply that human life as lived on earth can be confined to ends. It is right and healthy that each man should do his share of outward work. Even the Platonic sage had to return to the cave to enlighten his fellows, and still more the Christian thinker and the Christian saint have the duty of helping their fellow-men.

Nor are we asking a sensible question if we ask what is the most perfect form of life. There is only the most perfect life for A, for B, for C and so on. A man has to ask what is the best way for him to live, and that is an individual question with an individual answer. Hence it is important to avoid the sort of spiritual snobbery which regards the contemplative life as alone worth pursuing. Facile generalizations about the value of prayer do not always hit the mark. If a man is desperately in need of a fiver, you would be imprudent and, if he were quick-tempered, might even expose yourself to physical injury if you told him that you could do him more good by praying for him than by relieving his need.

Nevertheless, one has the impression that this sort of spiritual snobbery is not yet extinct. Most of us nowadays have made the acquaintance, in literary form, of the odd females whom the modern St Teresa discovered as her future companions when she entered the Carmel of Lisieux. What one wants to say about most of them is that they would have been much better women if they had had an honest job of work to occupy their minds and hands. It seems that entry into the more exclusively contemplative orders should be made very difficult indeed unless we are ready to incur the risk of having contemplative convents full not of mystics but of neurotics.

The average modern man, no doubt, has the opposite bias in favour of action. It is far easier to induce one's parishioners to undertake long and fatiguing labours for the Church than to lead them to reflect and to pray. And, especially since the invention of the motor-car, they seem to expect their pastors to spend their lives darting to and fro across country and turning up here, there and everywhere, without much regard to the spiritual value, if any, attained by this restlessness.

We have already alluded to the unfortunate divorce in modern times between popular spirituality and theological thinking. The moral of all these undue conflicts is to over-come the narrowness of mind which sacrifices one value to another of equal importance. As with the alleged antithesis of the sacred and the secular, so with the alleged antithesis

of contemplation and action, the genuine Christian ideal is
one of comprehensiveness and harmony, with a different application in detail to every individual. Everyone must reflect in
his individual way, everyone must praise God and want to
contemplate him in prayer, and everyone has his work to do.
We have enough to do in arriving at our own proper equation
in these matters without seeking to establish an order of
value in the appropriate contributions of others.

CHAPTER VI

SIN AND SINFULNESS

SIN AS A RELIGIOUS NOTION

When we speak of sin, we are usually seeing wrongdoing in a religious context. If I rob you, I do you wrong, and I can acknowledge this without introducing any but purely human considerations. But, if I call this a sin, I mean that I have not only wronged you but contravened an order of things which is established by God. This divine sanction has sometimes been thought of as depending on the arbitrary will of God, but this is incompatible with our sense of the intrinsic and objective nature of right and wrong. God himself cannot make right wrong or wrong right, otherwise he would contradict his nature as supreme intelligence. It is because he sees right to be right and wrong to be wrong that he commands the one and forbids the other. This is the doctrine of St Thomas Aquinas, and it seems quite evidently true on reflection.

It is, then, when we consider the difference between right and wrong in the context of the divine intellect and will that we think of acts as meritorious or sinful in the eyes of God. The distinction that we are accustomed to make between mortal and venial sin belongs not only to a religious context in general but is a part of the strictly theological or supernatural order. There are greater and lesser wrongs, but the distinction between mortal and venial sin is not simply one of degree. Mortal sin is a kind of wrongdoing which is incompatible with the continued existence of the infused virtue of charity in the soul, whereas venial sin does not destroy the bond of charity between man and God.

How this is to be explained is something which no theological thinker has ever made clear. When we say that mortal sin is a grave wrong recognized as such but deliberately perpetrated, we have obviously not said enough, for we have laid ourselves open to the question exactly how grave such a wrong must be. We could be asked, as indeed people have asked, exactly how much one must steal in order that this should be mortally sinful and, therefore, exactly how much one can steal while remaining comparatively unscathed in the region of venial sin. To such a question there is evidently no answer. The difference of a penny between one sum of money and another could not by itself entail the momentous distinction between mortal and venial sin.

It seems to remain that there is no final criterion except the criterion of charity itself. A mortal sin is an act which a man cannot do while continuing to love God; a venial sin is a momentary aberration from a love of God which continues. Could a fully deliberate refusal to do God's will be only a venial sin? Are venial sins always acts which we do with a divided mind? Then, is what we think of as objectively venial just the kind of sin which we easily or usually do with a divided mind? At any rate, when a moral theologian speaks of a kind of sin as objectively mortal, he must mean that it is the kind of act which calls for an unequivocal decision for or against the divine order, although there may in particular cases be extenuating circumstances of failure to realize its nature or of overwhelming impulse. There is certainly a personal equation to be taken into account. After all, sin and merit belong essentially to the intimacy of man's personal relationship with God. But we may be sure that the divine withdrawal of grace is not arbitrary. It is only that the divine logic, so to say, is more delicate than any human discrimination in perceiving what does and what does not entail the forfeit of the gift of charity.

GOD AND CONSCIENCE

The conscience is our power of judging what is right and what is wrong. It is in itself no more infallible than our power of judgement in any other sphere, but, as in other fields, our power of moral judgement can be improved by reflection and by the habit of following an unbiased conclusion. What, then, should we say of those, like Newman, who claim that conscience gives them a special kind of awareness of God? It might seem that there is nothing more divine or more indicative of the divine about it than there is about our capacity to do arithmetic. Of course, we may, like St Augustine, see our grasp of unchanging moral truths as well as our understanding of eternal mathematical truths as entailing the existence of an eternal mind as the necessary basis in reality of eternal truth, but this is not what Newman meant by his conception of conscience as the voice of God.

The essentially religious character of the idea of sin makes us see what Newman was driving at. What he meant was that he could not dissociate his sense of right and wrong from a sense of the possibility of sin. But a sense of the possibility of sin is a sense of our responsibility before God. Therefore the deliverances of Newman's conscience were inseparably bound up with a recognition of God.

The argument from conscience is not, then, a straightforward objective argument for the existence of God, like the argument to a first uncaused cause. It is rather an argument intended to show that we have an awareness of God, from whatever source this awareness may have originally come and however it may be rationally justified. As such its validity depends on psychological considerations. It was certainly valid for Newman, as he so eloquently tells us, but many men will say that their sense of right and wrong is psychologically independent of their sense of sin or even, if they are not believers, that it exists without any accompanying sense of

sin. Their testimony to their psychological make-up is equally
to be accepted.

SIN AND SINFULNESS

With a less than divine clearness of understanding we are
often hard put to it to decide exactly how full is our responsibility for our own wrongdoing. It is a great deal harder to
come to any decision about the responsibility of others. A
judge has to follow a conventional standard of average human
responsibility in order that laws may be enforced, but this
standard has to be admitted as susceptible of disproof in
particular cases. A confessor in the sacrament of Penance
can usually give help to the penitent without arriving at any
final judgement about the degree of the penitent's personal
responsibility for his sins, and this is just as well, for otherwise his task would be impossibly difficult. Without any such
function as that of the judge or of the confessor it is wiser
to abstain from even an approximate judgement. This measure
of agnosticism is the clearest foundation for the duty of
charity in our view of others.

It can be seen that this difficulty is acknowledged in Christian theology, for the simple reason that sin is extended to
cover cases in which wrongdoing is inevitable. Thus it is
said that we cannot in the present order of things fulfil the
substance of the divine law without grace and that, even with
ordinary grace, we cannot avoid all venial sin. If these are
genuine impossibilities, our responsibility for failure is less
than fully ultimate and personal, for, if it were, we could
avoid failure in any and every case.

Thus the acute sense of personal sin fades into a sense of
general sinfulness, and our power of discrimination is insufficient to draw a decisive line between them. In modern
English it seems not inappropriate to talk in this way of a
sense of personal sin and a sense of general sinfulness, the
latter being a recognition of the distance between our vague

and inconstant wills and the unchanging holy will of God. So we may suppose that, when St Peter saw the divine power manifested through the humanity of Christ and exclaimed "Depart from me, for I am a sinful man, O Lord", it was not that he was specifically conscious of this or that wrong act of his but rather had a profound realization of the distance between himself and the Incarnate Word. Our awe at the apprehension of the holy, as Rudolf Otto especially has pointed out, is closely akin to this general sense of sinfulness.

ORIGINAL SIN

Reflection on the general sense of sinfulness helps to make the idea of original sin more intelligible. Otherwise it seems strange, and indeed unfair, to the modern man to convict him of sin for something for which he has no personal responsibility. Man since the Renaissance has had a much more decisive sense of his individuality and what is due to it. Whatever else may be said about contemporary existentialism, the sense of creative personality is certainly enhanced by it. Hence, to talk about sin where there is no personal sin has begun to seem odd in a way in which it did not seem odd to our forefathers.

If we were going to invent a new theological vocabulary in English, it might be helpful to speak of original sinfulness rather than original sin, for the word *sinfulness* has vaguer and less personal implications. The point is that the social solidarity of the human race is such that the entry of sin into the world affected the position of all men in relation to God. We must, of course, avoid the really unacceptable extreme doctrines such as Calvinism. Original sin does not mean that we are all born with *personal* guilt and a *personal* liability to punishment. That would be plainly unjust. But it means that we do not possess the supernatural grace of God as our birthright; it is bestowed upon us through our incorporation in Christ. And even our natural powers of good are weakened by the infection of sin, although God must evidently make allowance in his judgement of us for our diminished responsibility for failure.

In this way, as Aquinas interprets it, original sin is not an absurdity or an injustice. Indeed, as many thinkers such as Newman have pointed out, some such condition almost demands to be invoked in order to make sense of the tragic history of mankind. Nevertheless it may look difficult to harmonize with an evolutionary account of the history of the world. For, while science tells us the story of a rise, Christianity involves us in a fall.

That people have not found these two world-pictures easy to combine is clear from the welcome recently given to the writings of Father Teilhard de Chardin. For, although Teilhard de Chardin was not remarkable for extreme accuracy and precision either as a theologian or as a scientist, he did succeed in showing a view of history which was both evolutionary and Christian. Perhaps the elements of harmony might be discovered on a less adventurous plane than his. If God has guided the world in its gradual development and interposed his creative power so that new levels of being might emerge, mankind was no doubt intended to develop from its primitive origins to the complexities of civilization. The possibility of the fall was implicit in the nature of man as a spirit struggling to emerge from an animal. The actual fall, the entry of sin into the world, must have enormously retarded man's development. Hence the long and obscure history of early man. But the divine plan was not to be thwarted. Christ was God's answer to sin. Development towards Christ and development from Christ put men back, although not without conflict, on the path which God intended for them.

The conflict, however, persists both in the history of mankind as a whole and in the history of each individual. The victories gained by grace are thus all the more precious. "Where sin abounded, grace did more abound" (Rom. 5. 20).

But we should have a very defective conception of the nature and conditions of the Christian life if we failed to take full account not only of our personal sins but of the original sinfulness from which Christ's redemption lifts us up.

THE CHRISTIAN LIFE AS A WHOLE

Gathering all the threads together, we may say that the Christian life transcends mere morality by raising it into the realm of grace, which prepares us for a supernatural union with God. At the same time it insists on the sinfulness of the human race, so that the need of self-discipline, which we have already seen to be a limitation of a too confident Christian humanism, is sharpened and intensified. Nevertheless, nothing that is naturally good loses its value in its supernatural order; the Christian ideal is not of a less but of a more complete man than the Greek ideal. The proper harmony of interests, human and divine, and the right proportion of contemplation and action have to be found by each individual in his own way, in accordance with his character and circumstances.

The final test is growth in charity, the love of God and our neighbour. Charity will not let us insist on our rights or confine ourselves to our strict duties; it always seeks the greater good. It overcomes any possible conflict between our desire for happiness and our readiness to fulfil God's purposes for us. It leads to joy, for we rejoice in the presence of the beloved, and God is always present to us. St Augustine's "Love, and do what you will" means that whatever course of action is really inspired by charity will be for the best.

CHAPTER VII

THE GIFT OF WISDOM

GROWTH IN THE CHRISTIAN LIFE

The multiplication of treatises on the development of the spiritual life has been a feature of modern times. This is consequent upon modern man's preoccupation with himself, for such works tend to be written from a psychological angle. The two great Spanish mystics, St John of the Cross and St Teresa, who described their own spiritual development with a degree of introspective detail hitherto unknown, belonged to the sixteenth century, the century of both the Reformation and the Counter-Reformation. While they belonged to the latter side of this great division, their insistence on psychological detail is simply characteristic of modern man.

They have had many imitators, not all, unfortunately but inevitably, of equal holiness or equal penetration. It is legitimate to confess a measure of fatigue with the modern proliferation of spiritual autobiographies and to greet with less than the maximum of enthusiasm the latest alleged revelations of Sister Esmeralda of the Five Wounds. Nevertheless, the real and great mystics are always instructive to read. Similarly, when a theologian of the spiritual life who is not himself a saint attempts to arrange the teaching of the spiritual masters in systematic order, the result is not always impressive or helpful. The obvious danger is that fragments of what is valid for different psychological individualities are blended together but fail to make a real unity. The outcome is a bewildering sort of mosaic without a genuine pattern. The saints, however different from one another and from ourselves, continue to be more instructive and helpful. In describing their pattern of life they can stimulate us to try to find our own pattern.

If we took the modern literature of the spiritual life at its face-value, we might be inclined to ask the older theologians why they produced so comparatively little of the same sort. One may imagine St Thomas Aquinas faced with the inquiry why he did not compose a *Summa Vitae Spiritualis* in addition to the two extant *Summae*. Might not Aquinas reply, first, that he thought it more important to deal with these matters in fully objective rather than psychological terms and, secondly, that, if we have this in mind, we might find some of what we were looking for in the *Summa Theologica* itself, especially, for example, in the treatment of the gifts of the Holy Ghost?

For the older theologians were accustomed to discuss the development of the life of grace in connection with the qualities which are named in the vision of Isaias as the prerogatives of the coming Messiah. "The spirit of the Lord shall rest upon him: the spirit of wisdom and of understanding, the spirit of counsel and of fortitude, the spirit of knowledge and of godliness (piety), and he shall be filled with the spirit of fear of the Lord" (*Isaias* 11. 2–3). If these are the qualities of the Messiah, the medieval theologians argued, they will be communicated in their degree to his followers. The passage of the prophet is evidently of a poetic character; the enumeration of the seven gifts is not intended to be a scientific classification of mutually exclusive qualities. Nevertheless, the way in which the scholastic theologians made these terms fit into their analysis of grace enabled them to say what they wanted to say about the development of human character under the influence of the Holy Spirit.

THE SIX LESSER GIFTS

St Thomas treats the gifts of the Holy Ghost in relation to the fundamental virtues as making man ready and willing to understand and to follow the divine will to which he already has the fundamental power to respond by means of the virtues. Hence the supernatural virtues cannot exist without some measure of the gifts, for a power completely devoid of any readiness to exert it would be a contradiction. Consequently we must think of the gifts as designating the degree of development of the virtues and not as something different from them. As baptism is the covenanted source of the supernatural virtues, so it must also be of the gifts, although we are right to call down the gifts in a special way at confirmation, when the candidate is intended to make the promises of baptism his own and to begin his life as a fully responsible Christian.

St Thomas attaches the gifts to the four cardinal virtues, in so far as they are lifted up to the supernatural order, as well as to the three specifically supernatural virtues. He does not find any gift to attach especially to temperance or the harmonious moderation of desires. Such a harmony in the primary human urges is presupposed to the development of grace.

To the virtue of fortitude corresponds, obviously enough, the gift of fortitude. That is to say, the full gift of grace does not only make a man capable of struggling against difficulties but enables him to face them with confidence and even with a special joy in thus serving the Lord and imitating Christ. It is not that he does not suffer, but now he is willing and ready to suffer for the sake of God and in accordance with his will.

To justice corresponds the gift of piety. Here we are using the word in the sense in which Virgil speaks of pious Aeneas on account of his faithfulness to his father and family and to the tradition of his race. The modern English word which comes nearest to it is *loyalty*. To have the gift of piety means, then, that we do not merely fulfil objectively our obligations to others but are loyal to our obligations. A genuine fellow-feeling with our family, our friends and, indeed, all men makes us willing and anxious to give them at least what is their due. Justice begins through piety to be transformed into charity.

Prudence is perfected by the gift of counsel. Moral judgement implies much more than the power to apply a rule to a particular case. An adequate moral judgement is based on seeing the case all round, in every relevant aspect; it implies, therefore, what we rather inexactly describe as imagination. The gift of counsel is just this power of moral imagination, bringing the fundamental power of moral judgement to bear on all the sides of the question before us. It makes us good counsellors both of ourselves and of others.

Faith develops into knowledge and understanding. Acceptance of God's revelation of himself is the first, but only the first, act of faith. To accept divine revelation and then to think no more of it is one way of hiding one's talent in a napkin and burying it away. The next steps are to acquire instruction and to make this instruction one's own. Thus St Thomas differentiates knowledge and understanding. Faith leads us to seek knowledge of the object of faith, but knowledge remains merely external without understanding. The whole difference between good and bad religious instruction resides here. Bad instruction is content with imparting knowledge, with providing the right words and the correct formulas. Good instruction is a progressive stimulus to the effort of understanding. If the theologian is pre-eminently the man of religious understanding, it is his job in the world to promote the highest possible measure of theological understanding among those who would not usually be described as theologians. Thus, faith, through knowledge and understanding, points towards wisdom.

The gift related to hope is the fear of the Lord. Here we have evidently no longer to deal with servile fear, the fear of divine retribution. Filial fear perfects hope because it means that we develop an ever greater horror of offending a loving Creator. We do not merely direct our lives towards God, but the thought of anything else gradually becomes intolerable and inconceivable.

THE SUPREME GIFT OF WISDOM

Wisdom, says St Thomas, is the gift of the Holy Ghost which perfects the supreme virtue of charity. The conjunction might seem odd. Charity means the love of God, but wisdom appears to be a quality of intellect. But what is the final test of the value of intellectual achievement? Surely, that it leads to a right attitude of mind and right action. And what is the final test of what we call love? That it is not mere sentiment but confers a special kind of rectitude of judgement. When we draw a hard and fast line between qualities of thought and qualities of feeling and action, we are somewhere on the route. In the end the highest qualities of mind and the highest qualities of heart must coincide, and it scarcely matters whether we speak of wisdom or of charity.

Even before Christianity Plato could tell us that the highest intellectual achievement was the vision of the Good, the possession in action as well as in theory of the supreme moral standard. The praises of wisdom in the sapiential books of the Old Testament present us with a similar harmony and unity of mind and heart. God we know to be supreme mind and supreme goodness in absolute unity. The best that he can confer upon his creatures is an approximation to that harmony and unity.

Therefore we pray to God, in the communication of the Holy Spirit, *da nobis recta sapere*, a phrase which is a crux for translators. Most commonly, when we use the prayer in English, we ask to be made truly wise, as if the phrase were *fac nos vere sapientes,* a translation which, however, has its justification in the connection of *sapere* and *sapiens,* and stresses that we are asking for the gift of wisdom. More literally, but in English rather oddly, we ask to be able to relish what is right. That, at any rate, however odd it may sound, explains what wisdom is. It is good taste on a divine level, that connaturality of mind and heart with God which banishes instinctively and at once whatever is inferior and unworthy of him. It is a refinement of mind which is based upon charity and grows in conjunction with it.

In the present context we need say no more. As charity is the supreme Christian virtue, so wisdom is the supreme gift of the Holy Spirit. God asks us, through the wisdom and charity of Christ, to grow into communion with the wisdom and love which is equally possessed by, and which unites, the Eternal Father, the Eternal Son and the Eternal Spirit.

CHAPTER VIII

THE CHURCH AS MORAL TEACHER AND LEGISLATOR

THE CHURCH AS MORAL TEACHER

That the Christian Church has the dual function of teaching faith and morals is obvious enough. For we do not attain salvation purely by religious observance; the moral aspect of all our acts is relevant to our relationship with God and, consequently, belongs to the concern of the Church. Yet we do not find a long series of solemn ethical definitions parallel with the detailed theological definitions which have been made according to need at various times in the history of the Church.

The reason for this is not really obscure. It is that Christianity does not offer us a new code of moral precepts. The law of love is the chief contribution of Christianity to ethics, but the precepts which are enhanced and enlarged by being brought under it are those which we consider, ideally at least, to be knowable by human reason without Christianity. When we defend them, we seek philosophical grounds for supporting them. Hence they have not needed to be set out at length by Church authority in the way in which the Councils have formulated the mysteries of faith.

Nevertheless, the Church has not been lacking in moral

exhortation on a less solemn level. In the early centuries we find a prolonged effort to enforce the strict Christian morality of sex and marriage against, first, the relaxed morality of classical times and, later, the primitive customs of the barbarian tribes which overran the Roman Empire. Once again, in recent times, it has had to be reasserted against neo-paganism. Slavery was too firmly entrenched in ancient society to be abolished at a blow, but gradually faded away under the influence of Christian ideals. In the Middle Ages we find the Church trying to mitigate the evils of the wars which she could not prevent and keeping guard against the economic ruin brought about by usury. Later we notice a series of condemnations of the practice of duelling. With the development of casuistry in the seventeenth century the Church had more than once to step in and correct the laxity of some moral theologians. In modern times, since Leo XIII, a series of encyclicals has dealt with the structure of civil society and the demands of economic justice, aiming at a happy mean between the extremes of *laissez-faire* and of Communism.

Apart from these special instances of authoritative moral teaching on the part of the Church a Christian moralist can have no doubt that he is an adherent of a tradition to which the whole history of Christianity is a witness. Although we regard the proper defence of moral principles as being based on philosophical reason rather than theological authority, we do not suppose that as individuals we have the task of constructing a deductive ethical system in a vacuum. Individual philosophical reflection can arrive at certain very general principles but can scarcely be assured of their detailed application. Hence philosophical ethics has to stop at some distance from the demands of concrete practice. It is enough if it turns out to harmonize with our accepted tradition as far as it goes. For the rest we look to a body of specific principles and attitudes which have gradually been developed and inherited, and whose full rational basis can hardly be explored by any individual thinker. In morals as in politics it is only reasonable to begin with a tradition upon which the critical reason exerts itself in cautious and piecemeal fashion.

THE CHURCH AS LEGISLATOR

To some it may seem repugnant to attribute a legislative function to the Church. For the value of religion depends upon its being freely and willingly embraced and followed, and the religion of love seems especially to go far beyond that concern with the limits of strict obligation which belongs to a legal point of view. Yet, in so far as some uniformities are necessary or desirable in the work of the Church, Church authority must have the power of making the appropriate rules.

Even the element of enforcement by sanctions cannot be denied to Church law. No doubt the main concern of the Church is with matters to which divine justice is alone appropriate, but the Church shows her abhorrence of certain acts by spiritual penalties such as excommunication and interdict and, in the case of clerics, suspension. We may well be glad that such spiritual thunderbolts are nowadays hurled about in a less carefree way than was customary in the Middle Ages, but they still exist as weapons for use in extreme cases.

Not even physical enforcement is necessarily out of place in Church law. We are not suggesting that there should be fines for failing to hear Mass on Sundays, but in matters which are more of means and less of primary spiritual ends the Church needs a power of implementing her decisions. If, for example, the ecclesiastical courts are hearing a case, maybe of nullity of marriage, they are badly hampered when, as in modern England, they have no power of enforcing the attendance of the essential witnesses. While the Church has no desire to maintain a private police force, the State should be willing to lend its assistance in appropriate cases.

Hence we need not be surprised that a vast body of canon law has developed in the course of history. The apostles already acted as legislators when, at the Jerusalem council, they decreed: "It hath seemed good to the Holy Ghost and to us to lay no further burden upon you than these necessary things: that you abstain from things sacrificed to idols and from blood and from things strangled and from fornication" (Acts 15. 28–9).   But the spirit of canon law should always be "to lay no further burden upon you than these necessary things". The Church does not want to become, or to seem to become, a legalistic institution. It is always a test of good and effective law that it should be capable of being kept relatively simple, and this is doubly relevant to canon law. If the Church's legislation is confined to the essential minimum, there will be no danger of the letter suffocating the spirit.

THE PROBLEM OF MORAL THEOLOGY

There has recently been a good deal of criticism of the writing of what is known as moral theology. Some of this criticism is misconceived, for it seems to ignore the purpose of this class of writing. A treatise of moral theology is neither more nor less than a handbook for confessors. This being so, it is inevitable that it should appear at first sight to be a rather odd amalgam of moral philosophy, sacramental theology and canon law. But a confessor has practical need of a mixture of these things, and it would be as unreasonable to blame the moral theologian for providing it as it would be to reject a practical manual for justices of the peace on the ground that it was not a shapely treatise on pure jurisprudence. Whatever we may suggest as possible improvements in the writing of moral theology, we must not forget its primary purpose.

We are right, however, if we are not too easily content with what the moral theologian offers by way of moral philosophy. Pure moral philosophy, as we have already remarked, can scarcely claim to be able to work out a complete and systematic ethical code. It has enough to do to establish a few basic principles and to analyse fundamental moral experience. Our detailed ethical code is the tradition of Christian ethics, but this, since it is not primarily an object of revelation, we seek to analyse rationally and to justify on a philosophical basis. It is important to acknowledge honestly how far precisely this analysis and justification is capable of taking us on each specific question. The fact that the conclusion is often taken for granted in advance may tempt the moral theologian to overvalue his arguments or to offer some pragmatic justification which is by no means free from the possibility of objection. We are often far from clear whether we are being asked to rely on an argument of principle, on the authority of previous moral theologians, or on the place which a conviction holds in the whole Christian tradition.

Some of the obscurities which demand a more persistent effort to dissipate may be indicated by way of example. How does the distinction between justice and charity compare with the distinction between commutative and distributive justice? And how precisely do variations in the duty of satisfaction or restitution follow from these distinctions? When should we say that a good end does not justify bad means, and when can we hold, for instance, that we can take the life of another as a means of defending ourselves? Why do we say that certain types of sin are always objectively grave? Can we make any final sense of the notion of a purely penal law, one which we have no moral duty to obey although we have a duty to pay the penalty for disobeying? What makes some moral theologians so accommodating in matters like mildly defrauding the customs or travelling first-class on the railway with a second-class ticket? The catalogue of large questions and small might be continued indefinitely, but these instances may suffice.

It would be rash to suggest that the moralists are wrong in their practical answers to these questions, but what is undeniable is that they are obscure and have for long been far too content with obscurity. Fortunately an active discontent with such obscurities has begun to manifest itself, and we may hope for a more speculatively satisfying moral theology in the future.

Casuistry is another element in moral theology which provokes divergent judgements. It is, of course, ridiculous to object to casuistry in general, for this would be tantamount to saying that moral reflection can be of no assistance in deciding what one ought to do in particular cases. If ethical thinking is going to be more than a doubtful theoretical luxury, it must reach as far as concrete fact. Nor have we now to be disturbed by those instances of lax decision which stimulated Pascal's wrath against the casuists of his day in the *Provincial Letters*. For the purpose for which moral theology is written some specimens of its concrete application are evidently desirable.

Casuistry, however, does need to be freed from a certain tendency to legalism. When we are dealing with questions of law, we have to ask whether a particular case comes under a general rule or not. If there is any substantial doubt, we have to decide in favour of freedom, for a man cannot be strictly bound by a doubtful rule. Purely moral decision is of a rather different sort. Here we have in complex cases a number of relevant considerations, and our task is to decide the relative weight of the reasons on either side and to conclude where our obligation, if any, resides. We have also to take the view of the greater good which may be attainable beyond what is of strict obligation, for our conduct will be ethically all the better if we pursue this. Hence anyone discussing a moral case is in a different position from one who is trying to settle a point in canon law. This has not always been adequately recognized. There has been a tendency among moral theologians to treat all cases as if they were questions in canon law and simply to ask whether they came under some general moral rule or not.

Another difficulty about moral theology is that it is perforce concerned first of all with what is of strict obligation, whether in terms of pure morality or in terms of canon law. This is another reason why the greater good sometimes receives less than its due share of attention. Evidently a confessor cannot command a penitent to do more than is of obligation. Nevertheless he should equally evidently encourage him to do so. Consequently moral theology has not done its job unless it is constantly issuing an invitation to a full positive development of the Christian life. It should not appear to be, as it has sometimes appeared to be, a mere series of prohibitions with an occasional indulgent exemption.

As we noticed earlier, these criticisms of moral theology as it has actually been cultivated have been increasingly made in recent years, and we may take it that these defects are on the way to be remedied. We need a moral theology with firm intellectual foundations, one in which a really ethical reflection predominates over merely legal considerations, and one which points to a complete development of the spiritual life.

CHAPTER IX

TOLERATION

THE PROBLEM

In selecting for discussion a few topics concerned with Christianity in its social aspect none seems more imperative than the question of toleration. The nineteenth-century liberal took for granted that a man enjoyed a right to freedom of thought and expression and to act according to his conscience. In our own century the rise of violently intolerant movements, such as Russian Marxism or German National Socialism, has reminded us that a retreat from liberal principles is still eminently possible. We have observed with dismay how easy it seems to be to dragoon large educated populations into mechanical conformity.

When we look back at the history of Christianity, we may also feel disturbed in mind. There have been so many instances of persecution of non-Christians by Christians, and more especially of dissident Christians by Christians in power. Dr Edwyn Bevan has remarked:

> When one compares the religion of the Western world after the establishment of Christianity with the Greek religion ... two great deductions have to be made from the benefits brought by Christianity. One is the promulgation of a doctrine that the great majority of the human race were doomed to eternal torment. ... The other deduction which has to be made is that the governing power now compelled men by pains and penalties to profess the belief of the Church. Even if the theory of the universe maintained by the Church was in itself a more

reasonable one than that of any Pagan Greek philosophy, the fact that men were compelled by force to profess it put a new unwarrantable constraint upon the human mind.[1]

Of course the tolerance of the pagan world may be exaggerated. Socrates suffered death for the freedom of his criticism of accepted views. Even Plato, although he was an admiring disciple of Socrates, could demand, in the moral legislation of the Tenth Book of the *Laws*, that citizens should carry out the prescribed religious observances of the State to which they belonged or undergo imprisonment or even death. Cicero cites the Roman prohibition of religions which had not received the explicit approval of the state: *Separatim nemo habessit deos: neve novos, sive advenas, nisi publice adscitos, privatim colunto.*[2]

But we do not improve the Christian case by dwelling on parallel instances of intolerance among the pagans. We must ask what is the historical truth about Christianity itself in this connection.

THE EARLY CHURCH AND TOLERANCE

When Christians were themselves a persecuted minority, they asked for tolerance in the name of a general principle of tolerance. Thus Tertullian says: "It is not the part of religion to enforce religion. A religion must be embraced by conviction and not by force, for offerings to the Deity call for consent from the heart."[3] And Lactantius: "It is not by killing the enemies of one's religion that one defends it but by dying for it. If you believe that you serve its cause by shedding blood and multiplying tortures in its name, you are mistaken. Nothing should be more freely embraced than religion."[4]

By the Edict of Milan Constantine proclaimed tolerance for

[1] Edwyn Bevan: *Later Greek Religion*, London, 1927. Introduction pp. xxxvi–xxxix.
[2] Cicero: *De Legibus* II 8.   [3] Tertullian: *Ad Scapulam* 2.
[4] Lactantius: *Div. Inst.*, v–20.

all religions, but this happy state of affairs did not last. When the emperors become Christian, they expected to have scarcely less sway over the Christian Church than they had had over the pagan Roman religious system. The emperor was accustomed to be Pontifex Maximus, and he was not willing that his authority should have a less sacred character according to his new beliefs. Hence the later Roman and the Byzantine emperors became the protectors of the Church in an ample and frequently embarrassing way.

By legislating against the pagan sacrifices and closing the temples or converting them to Christian use the emperors, without actually proscribing the ancient worship, made it gradually more difficult to be a pagan, and one feels a certain sympathy with a sorrowing pagan like Symmachus, who retained the feeling that the greatness of Rome was bound up with the worship of the gods and saw the objects of his hereditary veneration disappearing. An insensitive soul like Firmicus Maternus could write to the emperors Constantius and Constans "Come to the help of these unhappy people; it is better to save them in spite of themselves than to let them incur their own ruin," but it is important to realize that this was never the accepted Christian standpoint. The Church always upheld the principle that the faith could only be embraced freely. Whatever the later excesses of Christian rulers and even of individual Christian ecclesiastics, this has always been proclaimed as the principle of the Church. For this reason heretics were treated more severely than Jews or pagans, for heretics were held to have incurred obligations to the Church by their baptism and were arraigned for unfaithfulness to these obligations.

In this respect the outlook of St Augustine underwent a sad change. He was faced with the problem of the Donatists, a sect which had separated itself from the main body of the Church in North Africa after the end of the persecutions, when its founders had accused some of the Catholic bishops of having compromised their faith in the troubled times and had chosen new bishops of their own. Hence there had been rival successions of bishops in some of the African sees for the greater part of a century before the time of Augustine. Augustine at first upheld the principle that the Donatists should be brought back to unity by argument and persuasion. Eventually, however, the imperial authority was used to coerce them, and Augustine was persuaded to approve of their being coerced back into the unity of the Church.

Augustine says in his *Retractations* that he had held his earlier opinion because he "had not yet discovered either what harm they would dare to do if left in impunity or how much the application of discipline would avail to amend them." Now he says that he finds them glad to be converted, although they would not have come over unless they had been forced to do so, and he is willing to apply the words of the householder in the parable :"Whomsoever you shall find, compel them to come in." While he continued to protest against the application of the death penalty to heretics, he is prepared to accept any lesser measure of coercion.

Compelle intrare—these were destined to be fateful words. It would be difficult not to sympathize with the outraged eloquence of Gaston Boissier.

> In rereading these words, which have been so often quoted, I cannot suppress a feeling of sorrow. I think of the terrible consequences which have been drawn from them; I call up before my mind all the victims which they have made.... They were pitilessly applied all through the Middle Ages and caused so much blood to flow.... They had so taken hold of men's minds that no one protested against the use which was made of them.[5]

AQUINAS AND THE MIDDLE AGES

For the Middle Ages it will be sufficient to quote a thinker as representative and as enlightened as St Thomas Aquinas.

[5] Translated from Gaston Boissier: *La Fin du Paganisme*, Paris, 1913, vol. I, p. 77.

He discusses the relevant problems in the *Secunda Secundae*, qu. 10–11.

In qu. 10 art. 8 he asks whether infidels should be compelled to adopt the true faith. Here he asserts the principle that faith must be accepted freely. Hence Jews and pagans, who have never had the faith, must be left free to follow their convictions, although they may be restrained from interfering with Christians. Heretics, however, who have professed the faith in baptism, should be forced to observe what they have undertaken. In art. 11 he asks whether the religious rites of infidels should be permitted. While he grants a certain positive value to Jewish observance as prefiguring the New Testament, he regards other non-Christian forms of religion as simply evil. Hence, if they are to be tolerated, it is only for the sake of a greater good, for example, in order to preserve peace. In art. 12 he asks whether the children of Jews and other infidels should be baptized against the wishes of their parents. This he denies on the ground that it would tend to provoke an opposition between the child's natural allegiance to its parents and its acquired allegiance to the Church, and this would be a danger to faith. Parents do not, by failing to profess the true faith, lose their natural function of educating their children.

In qu. 11 art. 3 Aquinas asks whether heretics should be tolerated. It is evident that the people whom he has in mind are heretics of the first generation, people who were baptized into the true Church but have separated themselves from it. We may fairly conjecture that he would have judged somewhat differently if he had been thinking of people reared in an already established dissentient body. In fact, however, he compares heretics with coiners, since they produce false money in the spiritual order. The Church will exercise mildness, showing mercy to them once and again if they repent, but after that, if they fall away once more, she is entitled to excommunicate them and to hand them over to the secular arm for execution. Even then, he adds in art. 4, they should

be absolved on repentance, but they are still to be executed
as an example to others.

All this makes rather depressing reading as the considered
opinion of a naturally humane and objectively thinking man.
It is not that principles of moderation are lacking. Aquinas
upholds the principles that the faith should be professed
freely and that parents have a natural right to see to the
education of their children. Nevertheless, he allows very little
room to the possibility of good faith in dissentients, and his
whole exposition has a juridical flavour which seems to us
out of place in such matters. Yet we cannot understand the
Middle Ages unless we recognize that such an approach to
these questions was taken for granted. The dire results of this
outlook only became fully apparent with the division of
Christendom at the Reformation, when the now separate
Christian bodies began applying the full rigour of medieval
principle to one another and when it became possible for
secular rulers to invent their own form of Church and at
once to enforce its observance by pains and penalties.

THE BASIS OF TOLERANCE

It is again to be regretted that men learned the necessity of
tolerance more from weariness with strife than from any direct
moral insight. After a century of semi-political, semi-religious
conflict the religions of Germany were settled by the Peace
of Westphalia on the theoretically quite indefensible basis of
the choice of the local ruler. Religious minorities continued
to be persecuted, as were the Catholics in the British Isles and
the Protestants in France. It was supposed that there could
be no foundation for a stable polity if differences of religion
were allowed.

At last men came to realize that greater disunion was
caused by persecution than could possibly arise from religious
disagreement, and statesmen began to see that tolerance provided the only feasible means of peace. But the chief early

theorists of tolerance were men like Locke, whose theology was somewhat vague, and Voltaire, whose theology was almost non-existent. Among divines the Cambridge Platonists of the seventeenth century, especially Benjamin Whichcote, have an honourable place in the history of tolerance, but theirs again was a latitudinarian theology. Consequently, many of the characteristic arguments for tolerance are based on an absence of strong convictions. It remains a subject for discussion whether there is a sufficient theoretical basis for tolerance which is compatible with firm beliefs.

It would be regrettable if there were no more fundamental arguments in favour of tolerance than those advanced by John Stuart Mill in his essay *On Liberty*.

> First, if any opinion is compelled to silence, that opinion may, for aught we can certainly know, be true. To deny this is to assume our own infallibility. Secondly, though the silenced opinion be in error, it may, and very commonly does, contain a portion of truth; and since the general or prevailing opinion on any subject is rarely or never the whole truth, it is only by the collision of adverse opinions that the remainder of the truth has any chance of being supplied. Thirdly, even if the received opinion be not only true, but the whole truth; unless it is suffered to be, and actually is, vigorously and earnestly contested, it will, by most of those who receive it, be held in the manner of a prejudice, with little comprehension or feeling of its rational grounds. And not only this, but fourthly, the meaning of the doctrine itself will be in danger of being lost, or enfeebled, and deprived of its vital effect on the character and conduct: the dogma becoming a mere formal profession, inefficacious for good, but cumbering the ground and preventing the growth of any real and heartfelt conviction, from reason or personal experience.

Evidently the first two of these reasons will be the less effective, the more firmly anyone holds his belief to be true. The last two have a measure of practical validity, but we can scarcely ask a certain number of people to devote their energies to the propagation of error in order to make the holding of truth on the part of the others more lively and vigorous. We must ask whether there are reasons for respecting contrary opinion which are compatible with any degree of firmness of belief.

It seems that there we are. We might be inclined to assert that in any case what can be coerced is not opinion but the expression of opinion. Nevertheless, recent examples of what is horribly called "brainwashing" make us more cautious. Even though, however, something resembling a conviction can be produced by such means, we should recognize that such a conviction, being wholly irrational, is worthless. There can never be any justification for what is equivalent to pulverizing an intellect into subjection.

We can still ask whether we could be justified in preventing the expression of false opinion. A motive in the sphere of religion might be the protection of simple folk who could easily be led astray by specious argument, and such a relatively honourable motive has doubtless had its effect in history. Yet the only appropriate reply to reasoned argument is better argument. The forcible suppression of hostile argument for such a reason is precisely the kind of case in which Mill's third and fourth grounds for toleration find their chief application. We must respect the intellects even of simple folk. The case, of course, is not the same with incitements to violence, whether to a breach of the civil peace or to revolt against the State. We must all agree that such emotive propaganda can be justly suppressed, in spite of the practical danger that States may here abuse their power and extend suppression too far. We are not obliged to find a panacea for every possible aberration, for such a panacea does not exist. What is important is to uphold the principle that rational argument, even when we strongly disagree with it, should be treated with respect and should be answered by no less clearly intellectual a refutation. If error as such has no rights, sincerity cannot be denied its rights.

In the same way we should hold that a man has a right to act in accordance with his convictions as long as he does no harm to others. We should still, no less than the men of the Middle Ages, feel that a religion which involved human sacrifice ought to be suppressed! Even in the nineteenth century it was found impossible to tolerate the early Mormons with their doctrine of polygamy in the already established States of the Union, and they had to make their celebrated trek into the interior and to found a new State of their own. But we no longer, if we are reasonable, look on ordinary forms of religious practice which are not our own as evil. We look on them as lesser goods than the worship which we ourselves profess, but it is obviously good in its degree that a man should practice sincerely the religion in which he believes, whereas it is clearly evil that he should be made to take part insincerely in what he does not believe.

Thus there is adequate reason to uphold the tolerance of religious belief and practice as a theoretical principle in general and not only as a practical necessity in particular circumstances. Where the medieval theorists erred was in underrating the possibility of sincerely mistaken belief and in taking too legalistic a view of the claims of the Church on those who had become her members by baptism. We must acknowledge the periods of religious persecution as a blot on the history of Christianity. Fortunately those days are past. Now and henceforward the principle of religious toleration and of the toleration of dissentient opinion in general is to be seen not only as a matter of political expediency but as the only course compatible with the spirit of Christianity and the gospel of love.

CHAPTER X

THE BASIS OF CHRISTIAN
SEXUAL ETHICS

PREPARATORY CONSIDERATIONS

The purpose of this chapter, as indicated by the title, is to discuss the logical scope and force of the arguments by which defenders of traditional Christian sexual ethics are accustomed to support their recommendations. Although the tradition which they are intended to support may be historically described as Christian, these arguments are usually of a general philosophical character and might, therefore, be expected to make an equal appeal to persons of all religious allegiances or none. In actual fact we all know that they often fail to produce conviction. Here it would be naïve to underestimate the influence of contrary inclination, but it would likewise be rash to suppose that this is the only reason why our well-meant arguments are ineffective. Are the arguments themselves, at least as they are usually expressed, as watertight as we should like them to be? Asking this question must not be suspected of an intention of sabotage; if our weapons need sharpening, it is just as well to find out.

Before embarking on the main discussion I want to make certain distinctions which may be exemplified from other parts of the ethical field but will turn out to be relevant when sexual morality is discussed. No doubt there are many points on which right and wrong may be discerned by a simple examination of human nature and its essential demands. Why should we not lie to other people, why should we not maim or kill them? Because these are obvious ways of doing them mental or physical harm. It must be observed, however, that the generalizations which we make on these subjects are either tautologies or such as to admit of exceptions. "Lying is always wrong" is true only if we mean by it that an unjustified falsehood is always unjustified, which is not very enlightening. If we ask whether falsehood is always wrong, we have to answer that, although falsehood is *prima facie* wrong, it might be justified in special circumstances, as, for example, if there were no other way of protecting what ought to remain secret. Similarly, "Murder is always wrong" means that wrong homicide is always wrong. When we use the ethically neutral term "homicide", we must admit that, although homicide is *prima facie* wrong, it may be justified if it is an unavoidable means of self-defence or on the part of an agent of society like a soldier or an executioner. Our substantial or non-tautological moral generalizations are *prima facie* valid, but the possibility of exceptions has always to be considered.

Secondly, it can hardly be doubted that there are some moral precepts which might appear at first sight to belong to the purely human level but which really can scarcely be upheld without reference to religious factors. Why do we condemn suicide? No doubt it is *prima facie* doing harm to ourselves, but, especially if we believe in immortality, there might well seem to be cases in which we could judge that it was appropriate to transfer ourselves to another sphere of existence. Can we argue that we are depriving society of the aid and comfort which we owe to it? But sometimes we are likely to be of precious little aid and comfort to human society. It remains on reflection that, if we always condemn suicide, this is really from a religious motive. It is because we look on life as something given to us in trust by God for his purposes, so that it is for God, and not for ourselves, to decide when it should have an ending. Such precepts of natural religious morality have to be distinguished from precepts of human morality for whose support no appeal to the notion of God is necessary.

Thirdly, we must discriminate simple precepts of natural morality from precepts which presuppose the existence of social institutions. In so far as such institutions are regarded as demanded by human nature, these are still precepts of natural morality, but, if in an actual state of human society these institutions are not or are only imperfectly realized, the corresponding precepts are incapable of full observance. We may hold, for example, that there is a natural right to accumulate capital assets as private property, but it is a right which cannot be exercised or respected unless the social structure is such as to make it possible. If you are living in a Communist country, you may think that its social structure should be changed, but you cannot assert a right of property which the laws do not allow you.

THE MORAL PRINCIPLES

With these considerations and distinctions in mind we may embark on our proper subject. It can be assumed as a matter of elementary observation that, although sexual intercourse does not always result in procreation, its adaptation to this purpose indicates its most obvious significance in human life. Hence, in harmony with the ordinary opinion of mankind, we condemn solitary and homosexual activity as contrary to the manifest nature of sex. Although opinions may differ about the question whether such acts are in the concrete more often done with full moral responsibility or more often the result of a psychological obsession, no reasonable person has any doubt that they ought to be avoided and that the obsession, if such there be, ought to be overcome. We might well think ourselves entitled to go on and say that interrupted or obstructed intercourse must be condemned for precisely the

same reason, because it frustrates the most obvious significance of sex. Indeed some people are content to put the argument against artificial birth control just as simply as that.

But what exactly is the weight of this argument? It certainly establishes a *prima facie* case, but the solution of a
moral question demands that all the relevant factors should
be taken into account. *Prima facie* generalizations are, as we
have noticed with reference to truthfulness and to respect for
human life, in principle susceptible of exceptions. No plausible exception can be suggested in the cases of solitary and
homosexual activity; hence we may there legitimately convert our *prima facie* generalizations into strictly universal
condemnations. Before we issue a universal condemnation
of artificial birth control, however, we are logically bound to
consider the case that has been made for exceptions.

The commonest case in favour of artificial birth control
runs, as we all know, as follows. Circumstances frequently
arise in which the conception of children would be undesir-
able or even wrong. In such circumstances sexual intercourse
nevertheless retains its value as an expression of affection
and as promoting the interpersonal unity of husband and
wife. Hence, if human intelligence can devise means by
which this worthy end is attained while procreation is excluded, the act of intercourse is still morally justified.

At this stage we are inclined to answer that sexual intercourse is not a genuine expression of the unity of husband and
wife in independence of its primary significance as the means
of procreation. At once we are faced with the difficulty that
we accept the legitimacy of intercourse during the safe period,
intercourse in a naturally sterile union, and intercourse at an
age at which conception is impossible. In none of these cases
is intercourse a means of procreation, but we regard it as a
proper expression of affection between husband and wife.

A certain embarrassment in face of this difficulty seems to
be the explanation of why some moralists are reluctant to
admit that a desire to avoid procreation is ever fully legiti-

mate, whether the blame is to be put on individual husbands and wives or on social conditions. But it is really ridiculous when an otherwise meritorious writer remarks that "the responsibility for the lack of means to bring up a family lies at the door not of these parents, but of iniquitous industrial capitalism."[1] It is not the fault (or the merit) of "iniquitous industrial capitalism" that medical science has so progressed that the vast majority of children born are likely to survive and grow up. There was a time, no doubt, when infant mortality was so high that unlimited fertility was necessary in order to maintain the population. This is no longer the case, and modern parents have evidently to think of planning their families. The situation is common to every fully fertile union, quite apart from cases in which, for example, the life of the mother would be put in grave danger by another pregnancy and, consequently, the husband is bound to avoid giving his wife another child if he wants to escape incurring something approximating to the guilt of murder.

If, then, we admit the legitimacy of restricting intercourse to the safe period as a means of birth control but condemn artificial means of procuring the same end, we must find the point of the distinction between positive interference and letting well alone. At first, it must be confessed, this seems unduly reminiscent of the sort of morality described by Clough's well-known couplet:

> Thou shalt not kill; but need'st not strive
> Officiously to keep alive.

We do not judge, for example, that it is much more admirable to watch a person drown while callously doing nothing to help than it is actually to push him into the water. Is there an operative difference in our present case?

The point seems to be that, when there is no positive interference, sexual intercourse, even when it does not or cannot

[1] A. Bonnar, O.F.M., D.D.: *The Catholic Doctor*, 3rd edition, 1944, p. 75.

result in procreation, retains the ideal significance of a proper expression of affection between husband and wife, that is, between persons with the status of potential joint parents. For it is not the proper expression of just any sort of affection or friendship between man and woman. To suppose so would be to uphold promiscuity. There lies the fallacy of trying to justify it simply as an expression of affection. For, since it expresses the union of persons with the status of potential parents, interference with its natural consummation contradicts and destroys its essential moral character. No such contradiction arises when the act is naturally infertile, and its ideal significance remains intact. That is why there is in this sphere an essential moral difference between positive interference and letting well alone which it would be sophistical to try to make in other questions.

We must conclude, therefore, that the case for exceptions is not made out, since sexual intercourse cannot be justified simply as an expression of affection between man and woman but is a proper expression of affection between persons with the status of potential parents. Anything in the act itself which contradicts this destroys its moral propriety. This enables us to say with full meaning that procreation is the primary, and the expression of affection a secondary, purpose of sexual activity. The latter purpose is secondary and not co-ordinate, because it is never morally completely independent of the former, at least in its ideal significance.

Argument on this subject is, then, inadequate unless, first, the modern need of family planning is frankly admitted, secondly, it does not stop at a simple *prima facie* generalization about the character of sex but goes on to consider what case may be made for exceptions, and, thirdly, it makes clear the special moral effect in this sphere of the difference between positive interference and letting well alone. With this amplification of reasoning the traditional view vindicates itself as a precept of natural human morality. But we must admit that the necessary reasoning is somewhat elaborate for the man in the street, and we need not be surprised that, where inclination is so often at variance with principle, many people should remain unconvinced by reasoning alone.

Hence we should take another step and, using another point that we made at the beginning, transfer the question to the sphere of natural religious morality. For the rights and wrongs of the matter are considerably clearer when explicit reference is made to a Creator. The religious man sees his powers, as indeed his whole life, as gifts which he holds on trust from God and which he must administer in accordance with the will of his Creator. Reflecting on his sexual powers, he sees them as bestowed upon him to enable him to take his part in the work of creation itself. He possesses them for a purpose which transcends the purely human level, and he owes it to a superior to guard them for the purpose for which that superior gave them to him. They continue, on the human level, to express the affection of husband and wife, but their creative purpose has now a sacred character from which no one has a right to derogate for the sake of a purely human good. All this is natural morality, but it is natural religious morality, and it is from this point of view that the ordinary man will most readily see, and be stimulated to fulfil, his duty in the matter of sex.

It is intelligible, therefore, that those who do not share a religious view of the world do not pursue their reflection far enough to share this view of sexual morality. Differences on both matters are likely to remain roughly parallel in the modern world. We must reluctantly agree with Dr St John-Stevas that there is not sufficient agreement to make laws against the sale of contraceptives acceptable or enforceable in non-Catholic countries. For "laws embodying moral precepts are only enforceable if they are supported by a corresponding moral consensus in the community".[2]

---

[2] Norman St John-Stevas: *Life, Death and the Law,* 1961, p. 96. Cf. pp. 94–103.

THE CHRISTIAN LAW OF MARRIAGE

When we discuss marriage, we are discussing a social institution, and a few remarks on the method and scope of such discussion will amplify our third preliminary point. In the case of marriage Christians must reckon with the Gospel prohibition of divorce, which canon law applies in the form that all consummated sacramental marriages are indissoluble. It is intelligible enough that unconsummated marriages should be regarded as dissoluble, since physical union belongs to the completeness of marriage itself. That non-sacramental marriages, even though consummated, should be dissolved on occasion by the authority of the Church might suggest that the absolute indissolubility of marriage belonged only to the supernatural order. The tenor of the Gospel text and the tradition of the Church, however, point to the indissolubility of marriage as being part of the natural law, at least in the sense that only God or a divinely appointed authority has the right to dissolve a consummated marriage. Hence we are accustomed to offer not only theological but philosophical arguments for the indissolubility of marriage.

What sort of philosophical argument can we offer for a social institution? Evidently we do not perceive by a simple inspection of the notions of marriage and of indissolubility that the one entails the other. There is no logical absurdity in the idea of a marriage contract capable of dissolution or even of one which needed renewal after a stated period of time. The matter is logically more complex than are primary moral principles. *Prima facie* moral principles are such as to commend themselves on inspection, although, as we have seen, it is always necessary to consider possible cases for exception. In considering the appropriateness of institutions, however, we are looking for the most helpful social framework within which primary moral ideals can be realized.

In this sphere we must have recourse to reasons of general expediency. I speak of reasons of general expediency in contrast with reasons of particular expediency, which recommend particular courses of action in particular circumstances. An argument from general expediency is an argument from effects in particular cases intended to lead to an inductive conclusion that the best results are produced in the majority of cases by setting up and observing a general rule of a certain kind. About marriage, then, we argue that, although there are hard cases which, if they existed in isolation, might well call for a dissolution of the bond, nevertheless a high standard of marital relationship and the proper upbringing of the children are best ensured in the vast majority of cases by everyone entering marriage with the firm intention of making it a partnership for life. To say that marriage ought to be indissoluble is to say that the institution of indissoluble marriage can be seen on an adequate view of the facts to be one which conduces to the general good of human society.

The argument, therefore, demands no occult intuition into the nature of marriage and is compatible with the fullest recognition of the hard cases which result from it. Yet, as it stands, we must be content to admit that it is only a probable argument. The absolute firmness of Christian conviction on the subject rests on theological rather than philosophical grounds. In a purely philosophical context we are arguing to what law ought to be, and in this sphere it is unreasonable to ask for more than probability in any but the most general principles. It should be added that, in abstraction from divine law, a man can enter only into the kind of legal engagement recognized by the society to which he belongs. A British citizen, precisely as such, can enter only into a dissoluble union, for our laws recognize the possibility of divorce. A member of the Church is subject to an actual divinely proclaimed law, and it is in virtue of this that his marriage is indissoluble. If this principle is applied by the Church to the unions of all baptized persons, even if they are not members of the Church, this is because their intention to contract a Christian marriage is held to be operative although their awareness of its full consequences may be defective. It must be admitted that this entails another crop of hard cases among potential converts, but it is difficult to see how the Church could take any other line.

In a strictly philosophical argument for the indissolubility of marriage, therefore, we are arguing to what law ought to be rather than to what law is. In favour of a social institution we have to rely on reasons of general expediency which lead to probable conclusions. If we are content with this degree of rational assurance, we may well judge that our argument is very strong and is being daily confirmed by the results of easy divorce. As Christians, of course, we hold that God has proclaimed a law on the subject which he intended to hold in any condition of mankind, but we should be foolish if we claimed by ourselves to see its absolute necessity with a divine clearness.

SUMMARY

Reflecting, as we have done, on the two most disputed points in Christian sexual ethics, we can see how clearly they exemplify the difference made by having a religious background to morality. The whole subject will bring out this point even more fully.

When we speak of sex, in common with everything else which can be traced to a creative God, as having a certain sacredness in its religious context, we must take care that we are not taken to mean that, for a Christian, it ought to become a mere field of duty and not of satisfaction. That would be simply ridiculous and would justify the laity in taking an even lower view of the common sense of their pastors than they are already inclined to take. What we do mean is that, while losing nothing of its purely human significance and gratification, sex acquires another moral dimension as well from its relation to a divine creative purpose.

Hence it becomes something which we are not justified in adapting with a view simply to our individual human purposes. It is to be rightly used and rightly enjoyed within the context which safeguards its divine purpose, and that is within stable marriage and as expressing the meaning of marriage. And it is only if we adequately prize the proper use of sex in marriage that we can assign a suitable value to celibacy also, not as a general ideal consequent upon a Manichean contempt for our bodily functions, but as an exceptional form of life undertaken by particular persons for particular purposes. It is, indeed, becoming more and more evident that the whole matter is not enhanced in significance but becomes immeasurably cheapened when divorced from its traditional religious context.

CHAPTER XI

CHRISTIANITY AND WAR

GENERAL PRINCIPLES AND AWKWARD FACTS

Moral theologians have usually held that a just war is possible and have tried to formulate the conditions under which it is right to resort to arms. Warfare is just when it is the only available means of asserting or defending a right as between States and when the remedy is not likely to be worse in its consequences than the disease.

It has often been pointed out that the citizen is not usually in a very favourable position for assessing the justice or injustice of what his government proposes to do. If conscientious and not unintelligent German bishops, ready in the sphere of internal affairs to protest against the persecution of the Jews and the slaughter of mental defectives, could nevertheless exhort their flocks to support Hitler's aggressive foreign adventures during the last war, it does not seem that the citizen's judgement about what constitutes a just war is likely to be much of a check on a government which controls information and appeals to patriotic sentiment. Hence some more radical opposition to war might seem to be demanded from Christians if this scourge of mankind is ever to be abolished.

Nevertheless, it can hardly be asserted that the traditional principles of just warfare are wrong in the abstract, and it is ideally possible to arrive at a rational view of whether they apply in this case or that. People are on stronger ground when they suggest that the destructiveness of military weapons has reached a point at which the consequences of resorting to war must always be worse than any other alternative. War conducted with a full use of atomic weapons would be simply a war of obliteration, and might even lead to the end of the whole human race. Should we not conclude that nothing could ever justify a total war such as it would be under present conditions?

Before accepting this conclusion it is well to reflect that many people were saying something very like this in the years preceding 1939. Although weapons were then less destructive and less indiscriminate, they were frightful enough to arouse expectations of a similar kind to those which we have now. It is useful to reconsider what we thought then, in order to see how far our opinions were supported or reversed by events and to inquire whether what is new in the present situation should alter our conclusions. Hence I venture to reproduce, as a basis for renewing the discussion, what seemed to me to be the proper attitude to take up in 1937.

HOW IT LOOKED IN 1937

It is only too easy to understand why there has been so much discussion of the ethics of peace and war during these last months. In spite of the frightful lesson of the Great War, a lesson within the memory of all except the youngest, the nations seem more anxious to be at one another's throats than ever. Social reform must wait while armaments are piled up, and it will be difficult for people to resist the temptation to use these expensive toys before they become obsolete. In some countries, this is not regarded as a temptation at all but as an essential outlet for national vigour. Meanwhile nations are pursuing policies of economic self-sufficiency which will make it easier for them to go to war and might even seem to be aimed at making peace conditions so unpleasant that no one will hesitate, when a suitable moment arrives, to accept the risks of war.

What will the next great war be like? To judge from the last example, wars do not easily work out in accordance with plan, and glib prophecies in detail of the character of the next war may reasonably be distrusted. But it cannot be doubted that it will be far more terrible than the conflict twenty years ago. The hints which reach us from time to time of new arms and new methods of warfare are quite enough to disturb us, even if we do not go on to imagine what new horrors there may be of which no hint has yet reached the public. It will not be a question merely of the rise or fall of one State or another; it is not a rhetorical exaggeration to say that the survival of European civilization is at stake.

Hence it seems almost incredible that anyone at present should look at the prospect of war with complacency. Yet governments continue to preach militarism, and there are even independent thinkers who still find something thrilling and noble in the fighting instinct. The primitive emotions which glorify the sword are still strong enough to be extended to the modern warfare of aerial bombing and poison gas. If it were contended merely that the use of force is sometimes a regrettable necessity, there would be no objection to make, but an emotional glorification of the fighting instinct is another thing altogether.

It is sad, although not entirely unintelligible, that movements of national regeneration should be accompanied by a rise of militarism, but it is both sad and unintelligible that a thinker should not be able to discriminate sufficiently to admire the former without welcoming the latter. It ought to require no great effort of thought to make the conceptual discriminations needed in order to pass judgement on militarism. We are told that the combative instinct is natural, that it is a sign of life, that without its exercise men grow soft and corrupt, and that consequently war has certain good effects. It is easy to answer that natural instincts and manifestations of life require to be governed by rational and ethical considerations, that strength of character is not synonymous with a desire to throw the furniture about and to break one's neighbour's head open at the least provocation and that, even when evil incidentally produces good, it does not cease to be evil. It is equally obvious that the resort to force is of itself an evil which can be justified only by the necessity of removing a greater evil, and that the interests of a nation demand to be subordinated to those of the world as a whole. Therefore no case can be made out for that readiness to resort at once to force for the sake of purely national interests which is the spirit of militant nationalism.

But what is the use of reciting all these plain truths when they are listened to only by the already converted? They would be enough to oppose to a rational theory, but in fact they are opposed to an emotional instinct. When people are carried away by an emotional instinct, it is not sufficient to show reason to them; they must first be persuaded to listen to reason. With half the governments of Europe deliberately encouraging the warlike instinct and preventing their subjects from hearing anything which they do not wish them to hear, the chances of making the nations listen to reason on the question of war seem somewhat remote. At any rate, as the engines of war accumulate around us, we have the melancholy consolation of reflecting that militarism would be quite easy to refute if anyone would listen to the refutation.

The pacifist position deserves more serious consideration. In view of the probable character of the next war, it is not surprising that many lovers of peace should think extreme measures necessary, should regard any sacrifice as worth making in order that a nation may avoid war, and should preach pacifism as the proper attitude of the individual even when the State to which he belongs is already at war. It is not necessary to take into account the extreme position which repudiates the use of force altogether; we will deal only with the more plausible view that, under modern conditions, a just war between nations is impossible, and that consequently, should one break out, it is the duty of the individual to refuse to take part in it. It is suggested that the physical and moral evils necessarily entailed by any modern war are such that no conceivable good to be obtained by fighting, even by mere active resistance, could justify their being incurred. For war today can no longer be considered as a conflict between armies with incidental damage to non-combatants and to property in the area in which military operations take place. Aeroplanes and chemical research have changed all that. The next great war would seem likely to be an orgy of mutual destruction on the part of nations, in which men and women, young and old, will be indiscriminately involved, with a consequent impoverishment of every aspect of human life. If any stable government survived, it would probably be a military dictatorship. Hence the conclusion is drawn that a State ought to be prepared to make any concessions rather than go to war and that, even if war should break out, its citizens ought to refuse to fight.

Such an argument can no longer be dismissed as mere fanaticism, and it is not answered by pointing out that a just war is theoretically possible. What is disputed is precisely whether the conditions which justify fighting can be present today. If one suggested that, to the extent to which a war is unjust on one side, it must be just on the other, one might be accused of logic-chopping, although the point has a certain relevance. But, to deal with the matter more adequately, consider pacifism as a course of action for the individual, and take the case of a country which is attacked and is defending its rights. The members of a minority cannot possibly do any good by refusing to take part in that defence; they only do harm by making it more difficult for their country to maintain its rights. All sorts of things may be obscure in such a situation. It may be arguable that the country would have incurred less damage by submitting at once or even that some compromise might have been more equitable. The morality of particular actions which its defenders are called upon to perform may be debatable. But there is one thing which is clear, and this is that a community has decided to defend its rights by force, and that consequently those who belong to it and enjoy their social entity in it have the plain duty to act with their fellows in social solidarity.

Now take the case of the individual citizen in a country which initiates a war. Under modern conditions, as Pius XI said, "any nation so mad as to contemplate war would be guilty of monstrous homicide and almost certainly of suicide". If, when an aggressive government was seeking war, a sufficient number of its citizens could prevent war from breaking out by organizing to declare their refusal to take part in it, they would evidently be right in doing so. Some of those who have argued against pacifism have exaggerated the incapacity of the individual to judge the decisions of the State; it is clear that the citizen may sometimes recognize plain evil in the action of his government, in making war, as in other matters, and he has then the duty to refuse to co-operate. So, even, when war breaks out, he cannot take part in aggression which he knows to be unjust. But in a great war the matter is likely to be more complicated. Even the States which were guilty, or more guilty than their opponents, of seeking war will probably, once war has broken out, be fighting not simply for the accomplishment of their unjust aims, but for their own existence. Then the unfortunate individual citizen of clearer sight and better will than his government will once more have the duty of taking part in the defence of what after all is his country.

The greatest ethical attraction of the pacifist case is probably that of the ideal of non-resistance to evil. But it is one thing to be a pacifist on one's own behalf and quite another to be a pacifist on behalf of one's fellows. As St Thomas Aquinas puts it, not without a shade of irony, "not resisting evil may be understood in two ways: first, as condoning an injury done to oneself, and this pertains to perfection in so far as it conduces to the salvation of others; secondly, as bearing patiently injuries done to others, and this is imperfect or even vicious, if apt resistance is possible" (IIa-IIæ, qu. 188, art. 3, ad 1m.). There is a moral duty to co-operate with one's fellows in spite of their muddled views and mixed motives. Co-operation with evil has, of course, to be excluded, but the defence of rights by force, whether it be the most advantageous policy in the circumstances or not, cannot be accounted as evil. So, if his fellow-citizens have decided to defend themselves against a declared enemy, a right-minded man does his job with the rest. So also, during peacetime, he takes his share in reasonable preparation for a possible future need of defence.

Individual pacifism, therefore, is not the way out of our present dangers and embarrassments. It might still be argued, as Lord Russell argues, that States ought to adopt a pacifist policy and to be ready to make any concessions rather than risk the horrors of a modern war. Certainly any ruler who pursues an aggressive policy is more monstrously guilty than ever before. But it is going rather far to say that the least harmful answer to the threat of violence is submission. If peaceful nations declare their readiness to surrender and make no active resistance to any sort of outrage, this is merely an invitation to the militarists to do their worst. The logical conclusion of such a state of things is that the most unscrupulous set of hooligans automatically takes charge of the world. Surely it would be better to go down fighting than to accept the kind of world which would result. The principles of non-resistance which might be followed by a perfect individual on his own behalf cannot be applied without modification to a community. The actual members at any moment of a worthy community are the trustees of a set of values which do not simply belong to them, because it is their business to preserve them and hand them down to those who come after them. Moral and cultural values are not created by physical force, but they are dishonoured if they are never defended by physical force, and a community whose organization enshrines values achieves a greater value by resisting, even to the point of facing extinction, rather than submitting to their loss or impoverishment in face of a threat of violence.

A country, therefore, which cherishes its national heritage ought to be ready to defend what is worth defending in it. In England today we need to make up our minds about what is worth defending, for to risk a modern war for an object of no importance would be inexcusable. We do not want to be pushed into war for individual commercial and financial interests; it is the suspicion of this which gives pacifism much of its force. We have also to recognize that, whether by accident or by design, we have become possessed of a very considerable part of the world, and we shall have no excuse if we make enemies by refusing to allow other nations their fair share. But within these limits, and without any recurrent inclination to chant *Rule Britannia,* we may soberly hold that the English tradition deserves to count for something in the world and that it is our part as men to see that it does so.

Yet in spite of the regrettable necessity of taking measures for national defence, there is a higher ideal to be kept alive. It has become almost a commonplace to say that the League idea is discredited. Certainly the existing League of Nations, with its record of inconsistency and failure, is not an impressive object to contemplate, and it would be better to abandon it frankly than to maintain it as a pharisaical mask for an alliance between England, France and Russia. But is the League *idea* discredited? On the contrary, something of the kind must eventually be made to work if there is to be any hope of lasting peace. Love of country, good though it is in its order, demands to be subordinated to the love of mankind. When States could be more or less self-contained, there was no imperative need to translate this higher unity of the human race into terms of political organization. But the world is too much of a social and economic unity nowadays for it to be safe to dispense with an international authority. No multiplication of pacts, treaties and gentlemen's agreements makes up for the absence of some real authority in international affairs. We do not want a world-state, for a State means a highly centralized organization, and the modern national State is already over-centralized. We need to develop the conception of a hierarchy of authorities, which are all genuine authorities in their proper spheres and not merely executive branches of the central State, and this under modern conditions ought to culminate in a confederation of States with power over international relations and the means of enforcing its decisions through a control of the air. Respect for the integrity of Notting Hill at one end and respect for the integrity of the world at the other, but no Napoleons.

In the present state of the world, with its complete absence of common principles, it seems idle to dream of such a consummation. Bergson's contention that there is a gulf between adhesion to an exclusive group and the love of mankind, *morale close* and *morale ouverte,* is only too much in accordance with the contemporary facts. But this is not a permanent necessity of human nature, and so it is worth taking its supersession as a long-distance objective, an ideal to be kept alive by the *cives præclari* during this period of conflict.

Meanwhile, people cannot afford to wait until the world comes round to their way of thinking before they set out to reach whatever modest degree of genuine international co-operation may be possible. Christians cannot abdicate their part as citizens of the world because the world is so little Christian. Since Christianity is the universal religion, the Catholic and medieval ideal of the unity of Christendom is the translation into a higher order of the ideal of the unity of the world. In that order the ideal could be more nearly realized, but even a distant approximation to it on a secular basis is worth striving to bring about.

These are dull and conventional reflections, no doubt, and they offer no short cut to a better state of things. They would not be worth making if they were not frequently forgotten. But at a time when pacifists tell us that we must surrender to the new barbarians, and militarists urge us to glorify our attempts at collective suicide, a reminder of the basic morality of "my station and its duties" is not beside the point. A man is born at a determinate time and in a determinate place, and he has to make an imperfect best of his actual circumstances, whatever they may be. He cannot simply reverse the influence of the foolishness and the wickedness of the past; he can do something, if he will, to lessen it. But he will make no contribution if he either yields himself to uncriticized emotional instinct or withdraws in disgust from the confused affairs of his fellows. He has a plain job to do both as a citizen of his country and as a citizen of the world; whatever may happen to him in doing it, the individual has a reality and a value transcending the accidents of the world, and through his grasp of this he may attain to serenity.

WHAT SHOULD WE THINK TODAY?

There is at least one obvious change in the atmosphere of thought since 1937. No one any longer thinks of glorifying war as a field of development of the military virtues. It is not that courage and endurance and self-sacrifice have ceased to be virtues, but the individual now counts for so little in relation to the destructive power of applied science that war must appear predominantly as a frustration of individual purpose and individual achievement. Any desire to sing about the happy warrior now seems intellectually frivolous and morally oblique.

It is also evident that our worst fears were, fortunately, not justified by the war of 1939 as it was actually waged. There was less sheer destruction than we expected. But we should not omit to consider how very near our worst fears came to fulfilment. The war came to an end only just in time before the final weapons and methods used by both sides revealed their full consequences. If the Germans had had another year to develop and use their retaliatory weapons, and if we had

had another year to practise the obliteration bombing of German cities and had dropped more than two atomic bombs on Japan, our previous more pessimistic prognostication would have been amply verified.

At any rate there is now no further doubt possible. If another general war occurs and is waged with the full resources of destruction at the disposal of the United States and Russia, no fears will be exaggerated. What, then, should we think and do? Are the consequences of unlimited war now such that it will always be preferable to submit to any evil or any oppression rather than to engage in it?

We must, of course, distinguish between questions of practical politics and the strictly moral question. It becomes increasingly clear that no other State has the area and the resources to compete with the United States and Russia in the development of atomic weapons. However mortifying it is to our national pride, we must admit that our British claim to possess an independent deterrent becomes an increasingly hollower bluff every day. We have really no alternative between collective suicide and Mr Pickwick's practical, if unheroic, policy of shouting with the crowd or, when there are two crowds, shouting with the larger one. No government is likely, or has the right, to call on its citizens to accept collective suicide rather than to give in.

But that is practical politics. The moral question arises when a State has a chance of surviving and of coming out better than its adversary from an atomic war. Could it then be morally justified in using these means of mass destruction? It is true that their possession by both sides has been and is an obstacle to wars breaking out. Yet they cannot be pragmatically justified simply because the mutual threat makes their use less likely. A threat implies a hypothetical intention of using them, and this intention has to be morally assessed.

Some would say that they are intrinsically evil in the strong sense that they cannot have any morally justifiable use. That they are immense evils in a less strong sense is evident,

but are we entitled to say *a priori* that there is no greater right
or obligation than the obligation not to use them? This type
of absolute ethical assertion is not easy to make. It is usually,
at any rate, by a reflection on possible exceptions that we
come to a conclusion whether there are any valid exceptions
to a moral rule or not. When we consider the duty not to
take the life of another human being, for example, we usually
admit exceptions where a man is acting as the agent of human
society or where no other form of self-defence is available.
Is it so clear that we are strictly bound to avoid the mass-
destruction involved in a full use of atomic weapons if there
is no other way of asserting a right to the freedom and institutions which we prize?

It may be said that warfare is tolerable only when attack
is confined, as far as possible, to military targets. No doubt
the distinction between combatants and non-combatants is
a salutary one which has done much to humanize warfare
in the past and is by all means, if possible, to be upheld. Yet
it is largely a conventional distinction. There is a sense in
which everyone is at war when the nation is at war. This
distinction, therefore, seems insufficient to found an absolute
moral rule.

But is not this sort of cold-blooded reasoning, it will be
said, precisely the kind of thing which brings the armchair
moralist into discredit? Could any genuine Christian face the
decision to obliterate a whole city and its inhabitants without
recoiling in horror? There, perhaps, is the point. For the
essence of Christian morality lies in the law of love, in a
readiness to go beyond what can be established as absolute
obligation. The Platonic Socrates had already argued that it
is always morally better to suffer evil than to do it, but it is
above all in the Gospels that this is put forward as a general
ideal. Even though, when we are thinking in terms of strict
rights and strict obligations, it may be impossible to establish
that full atomic warfare must be morally excluded when it is
the only possible form of self-defence, we cannot imagine

Christ as doing anything but inviting us to submit rather than perpetrate such horrors.

It seems to me, then, that the Christian is on his proper ground when, instead of trying to establish a strict and fundamental moral obligation to avoid such means in any circumstances, he appeals to their obvious incompatibility with the love of our neighbour for God's sake as a Christian ought to have it. Whatever may be the case on the plane of strict obligation, it is evidently a greater good to give in rather than to be responsible for so much harm to others even in the best cause. This is the principle which a Christian is invited to apply in his own case when he is urged to turn the other cheek, and he may well urge it on the whole nation or community to which he belongs.

A whole nation, however, willing to act in full accordance with the Christian law of love is an unprecedented feature in human history. Even nations ready to fulfil all their strict obligations in the international sphere are rare enough. In any case the action of a political society is limited by what is legally enforceable, and only what can be acknowledged as strictly demanded is an acceptable matter of legal enforcement. Hence, even in the most favourable circumstances, there would seem to be an inevitable gap between the possible range of political action and the full realization of a Christian social ideal. The latter can only come to be through the voluntary work of individuals. A relevant analysis of the situation was offered recently by Professor John Wild in the second part of his *Human Freedom and Social Order*.

It appears, therefore, that there is bound to be a certain tension between the social ideal upheld by a Christian and the common action of the political society to which he belongs. Does that justify him in opting out of his social obligations? Even in the tragic circumstances of today that does not seem to be any more the right solution than it was a quarter of a century ago. The Christian has not to wait for the perfect society but rather to make his contribution to the imperfect society in which he finds himself. He can work for peace without finding it necessary to be a pacifist on principle, and can find ground for hope in the common human instinct of self-preservation as well as in the higher moral ideal which he is bound to uphold.

CHAPTER XII

CHRISTIANITY

AND POLITICS

THE SCANDAL OF CHRISTIAN CONSERVATISM

Those keen progressives who interpret the human problem mainly in terms of politics and economics, and look to social changes for the salvation of man, must, if they are honest, regard the New Testament as a highly pernicious collection of writings. The Jews were living unwillingly under foreign domination, but Christ refused to lend himself to their national aspirations and told them to "render to Caesar the things that were Caesar's". Slavery was an established institution, but, although St Paul told his converts that "in Christ there is neither bond nor free", the practical counsel of St Peter was that slaves should "be subject to their masters, not only to the good and gentle but also to the froward". Even for the free, life was difficult and uncertain, but Christ himself simply told them: "Be not solicitous for your life, what you shall eat, nor for your body, what you shall put on."

The Gospels having been interpreted in so many different ways, we may be prepared to hear that they have even been construed as if they were primarily a contribution to social ethics, but it is only necessary to read them to see that this is futile. Hence it is not astonishing that violent political changes of whatever kind are usually accompanied by attacks on the Christian Churches and clergy; the crop of martyrdoms in our own time has not been small. Sometimes, when people read, for example, of the Spanish clergy massacred by the revolutionaries, they raise themselves from their armchairs sufficiently to remark that, after all, boys will be boys and, in any case, the clergy were probably not all that they ought to have been. The author of the Book of Wisdom seems to have foreseen the situation. "These are they whom we had some time in derision and for a parable of reproach. We fools esteemed their life madness and their end without honour. Behold how they are numbered among the children of God, and their lot is among the saints."

Of course, Christians, clergy and laity, never are all that they ought to be, but, besides that murder seems a somewhat excessive requital for their shortcomings, it is hardly necessary to look to these for an explanation of the awkward facts. For the very existence of the Church of Christ, whatever the character of individual Christians may be, is a standing rebuke to human pride and violence, to all the passions which find freer play in revolutionary times. More specifically, it is a standing reminder that the salvation of man does not come from politics, that there is one thing necessary and it is not to be found in a political or economic system. The Christian Church by its very nature proclaims to men the text which St Ignatius of Loyola dinned into the ears of St Francis Xavier until he persuaded him to join in the foundation of the Society of Jesus in order to help in meeting the first crisis of the modern world: "What doth it profit a man, if he gain the whole world and suffer the loss of his own soul?"

That, after all, is what most fundamentally annoys the man whose whole hope is in political activity. Here is a body calmly asserting that his activity is not of the first importance, that there is something else of which mankind has greater need. And his annoyance is all the more intensified by the suspicion that this may be true. Therefore, away with the Church! *Écrasez l'infâme!* Or else, more mildly, he demands that Christians should drop their ancient cry, should adapt themselves to modern conditions and preach whatever temporal gospel is most in favour at the moment. We begin to see the point of Pius IX's emphatic denial in the Syllabus of 1864 that the Roman Pontiff can and must reconcile himself and come to terms with modern civilization and progress. For the pope and the Church exist in order to bring before men's minds a truth which is not in the least affected by modern civilization and progress, and is exactly the same now as it was nineteen centuries ago.

This is not the place to discuss whether the Christian faith is true or not, but at least it should be clear what sort of thing it claims to be. It is not primarily an ethical system, even when coupled with the broad-minded admission that there may be a God. It is a religion, claiming to bring men into communion with God, who made them and for whom alone they exist. It centres round the Incarnation of God the Son, made man for us. Through incorporation with Christ in the Church of Christ men are reconciled with God and gain eternal life. This doctrine, when its rational grounds have been studied, may be believed or not, but people should at least refrain from insulting Christianity by maintaining that it is really something other than what Christians from the beginning have held it to be.

If Christianity is true, it must be frankly admitted that it matters rather less than it would otherwise matter whether in this world you are rich or poor, whether you receive justice or injustice. But it does not follow that this does not matter at all. Christianity, for all that it is not revolutionary and does not set politics in the highest place, is yet relevant to the temporal order, and has in fact, during the course of its history, worked gradually and unobtrusively towards human betterment. Now, therefore, that we have made our protest against the ignorant tendency to judge the Christian Church by the degree to which it can be subordinated to fashionable political ideals, we can permit ourselves to describe the relevance of Christianity to politics.

THE DIGNITY OF THE HUMAN PERSON

It would be beside the point to speak of the contributions which Christian thinkers, such as St Thomas Aquinas, have made to general political theory, for these were founded upon common human reason, and there was nothing specifically Christian about them. The Christian Church does not uphold any single political system but accommodates itself to many forms of secular government, even when they are highly imperfect; it is ready to acknowledge any State which does not forbid it freedom to fulfil its spiritual purpose. It is not the business of the Church to issue pronouncements on purely political questions as such, nor would the clergy make proper use of the pulpit to air their political views. A cleric only makes himself ridiculous by attempting to dogmatize to his people on matters in which his standing is no greater than theirs. He has the same right to hold political opinions as any other citizen, but to proclaim them is not part of his ministry and should be reserved for other occasions.

Christianity is much more concerned with producing the kind of man who will conscientiously play his part in any tolerable system, whatever that system may be, and it is concerned, too, with the idea of man which statesmen and legislators should have in mind, if their decisions and laws are to be satisfactory. The Incarnation is relevant here, when we consider how it has enhanced the dignity of human nature. The individual human nature, body and soul, which was assumed by the personality of the Divine Word, is of the same specific type as that which all men possess in all nations and races, of all degrees of intelligence and cultivation. In the most famous of his Christmas homilies St Leo brings out the relation of human dignity to the Incarnation: "Acknowledge,

Christian, thy dignity; remember of what head and of what body thou art a member."

For the result of the Incarnation in those souls which are incorporated with Christ is the supernatural life of grace, whose consummation is that intuitive knowledge of God which is the state of heaven. The goal which the Christian faith puts before all men without exception is an intellectual consummation; it is to know God as he is in himself. Hence, whatever men may seem to be, however little, in the common phrase, there appears to be in them, the Christian view enjoins a respect for every individual instance of human nature which could not be equalled on any other basis. Even here, in the stage of preparation, nourished for eternal life by the body and blood of Christ, the Christian person must be given a value in the eyes of men which is due to the value which he has in the eyes of God.

This is the man for whom legislators draw up their codes and statesmen make their decisions. This is the man who is often treated as cannon-fodder or as a guinea pig for social experiments. But, if the Christian belief is true, consider the sacredness of every individual human life and destiny. That is something to which the Church has the right and duty to summon the attention of governments.

The Church, therefore, proclaims to governments the sanctity of human life, even of the insane and mentally deficient, even of helpless invalids and unborn infants. It insists that effort should be made to provide men with the natural conditions in which they can fittingly fulfil their supernatural end. It exhorts men to settle their differences peacefully and to have towards one another that Christian charity which transcends human philanthropy by being a sense of fellow-citizenship in the city of God. All these are among the conditions of a sound temporal and political order, and their necessity is put in a clearer light by the Christian doctrine of the dignity of the human person and his vocation to the supernatural life.

CHRISTIAN REALISM AND SIN

While the Christian view of human dignity is thus relevant to politics, Christianity is not Utopian. It does not believe that a perfect system would make man perfect. It does not hold that, if material conditions were improved, men would at once become virtuous. The Christian doctrine of sin is, in fact, equally relevant to politics.

There is a great deal of Rousseau left in the contemporary climate of opinion. If, as Rousseau thought, it was only social organization which made men bad, the obvious remedy, since it was impossible to revert to noble savagery, was to reorganize society in a better way. The first attempts, with the French Revolution and the Napoleonic wars, were scarcely encouraging, but men were not yet daunted. All through the nineteenth century liberal thinkers tended to believe that Utopia was around the corner. A few more changes to be made, a few more shackles to be removed, and all would be well. Even the usually hard-headed Karl Marx betrays a similar naïvety, with his belief that, when the proletariat had shaken off its chains, the State would be no more and a golden age would begin.

It might well have been thought that such hopes could scarcely survive the events of the present century, but they are not dead yet. There is still the longing for a social panacea, and the belief that it will be found, even that, in some new system or other, it has been found. Perhaps the ghastly realities have made it only more inevitable that men should take refuge in dreams. At any rate the ghost of Rousseau still walks, and inspires a host of sentimental idealists who continue to look for a secular millenium.

The Christian is not less anxious to improve the conditions of society, but he takes a more realistic view of its prospects. Human nature is essentially good, but it is infected by sin and prone to sin. There is perhaps no Christian doctrine which more repels the typical modern man than this. He wants to blame all his failures on conditions external to himself, or, if he constructs a new morality, he consecrates his vices and sets his moral ideal so low that it is almost impossible for him to fall beneath it.

St John represents the Christian opposition when he says that "all that is in the world is the lust of the flesh and the lust of the eyes and the pride of life". The human race took a wrong turning at the beginning and separated itself from God. The evil of the past continues to have an effect in the present, and our own personal failures are added to the hereditary burden.

God has provided a remedy for this in Christ and in his Church, but it is not a remedy of which all avail themselves. Very few, in fact, avail themselves of it to any full extent. There is always an antithesis, as St Augustine traces at length, between the world and the Church, between the city of this world and the City of God. Sometimes the antithesis is softened, sometimes it is more acute, but it is always there. We may hope that things will be better; we cannot expect that evil will disappear.

Hence the Christian faith, with the highest possible view of the dignity and the destiny of man, insists also on some less palatable truths. Without grace man cannot long continue to observe the whole of the moral law. If he relies solely on himself, his moral practice will decline and his moral ideal will sink. The contemporary world provides a good deal of material for an experimental verification of these doctrines.

The Christian doctrine of sin is, consequently, highly relevant to politics. The Christian is not less shocked than the secular humanitarian when he reads of murders, atrocities and concentration camps, but he is perhaps less surprised. That is just the issue to be expected of the pride of life, when it is fully indulged. Man is capable of great good, but he is also capable of great evil, and it is not only external conditions which make him evil. He has a source of weakness within him, in the frailty of his will, which, although he can turn it to good, he so often directs towards evil.

The Christian, therefore, takes a balanced and realistic view of the possibility of social progress. He understands that great effort is required, not only to make things better, but even to prevent them from becoming worse. He is ready to make the best of much that is very imperfect in the world about him, because he knows how easily human conditions might be made a great deal less satisfactory. He is suspicious of Utopian schemes which involve the previous uncertainty of vast social changes, because these promises of felicity do not correspond with the facts of human nature, and he fears that their whole result will be an upheaval with a further deferment of the promised happiness.

Nevertheless, the Christian does not, or at least should not, succumb to the opposite extreme and supinely accept things as they are. He is, or at least ought to be, a social reformer, even though in a more modest way and with more modest hopes than the noisier Utopians who surround him. His very conception of the dignity and the destiny of human nature must make him anxious for conditions of society which respect that dignity and make it easier for that destiny to be fulfilled. If he rejects the idyll of Rousseau, his is not the cynicism of Hobbes. The Christian is a realist in politics, because he takes into account both the splendour of human capacity for good and the enormity of human capacity for evil.

THE IDEA OF CHRISTENDOM

There is one vexed department of contemporary political thought to which Christianity is especially relevant, and that is the field of international relations. In earlier times it was inevitable that there should be separate governments even for quite small areas, like the city-states of ancient Greece. The religions of these ancient states were also their own; each city and tribe had its gods. When one city or tribe warred with another, their gods also were pitted one against the other. There was hardly a conception of any moral duty as being owed to a man of another state or race. When we look at thinkers as enlightened as Plato and Aristotle, we find that, while they had some notion of a community of the Greek race, the barbarian was a being whose treatment lay completely outside the ethical sphere.

The ideal of the brotherhood of man was born with the Stoics. Every man was some participation of the cosmic Logos, and so all men had a certain unity. The willingness to extend the privileges of citizenship in the later Roman Empire owed something, no doubt, to Stoic ideals. At the same time, however, a much stronger force had begun to work in the same direction.

The Jews, as we see them in the Old Testament, were certainly not the least nationalistic of peoples. Yet their religion had a peculiarity which prepared the way for something different. Yahweh, the God of the Jews, was not merely the god of a single nation, fighting with it against other gods of other nations, but he was the God of the whole world. When the Jews were defeated and oppressed, it was not Yahweh who was beaten, but rather Yahweh, on account of the sins of the Jews, bestowed the victory upon their adversaries. The time would come when Yahweh would assert his lordship over the whole earth and when, as the Jews thought, all nations would submit to them and look to Jerusalem as their centre.

Christianity came as a spiritual fulfilment which transcended the crudities of Jewish messianic belief. The Jews were not to dominate the world, but Jew and Gentile were to be as one in the kingdom of Christ. It was not to be a universal empire but a universal Church. Hence the apostles and their followers went forth to convert the world, both inside and outside the Roman Empire, and firmly rejected all national religions and national gods. Their aversion from the Roman imperial cult was, in fact, the reason why they were regarded as potential rebels and subjected to spasmodic, but sometimes fierce, persecution during the first three centuries of our era.

When Christianity became the official religion of the Roman Empire, it did not cease to be a world religion, nor, when the Roman Empire broke up, was the unity of the Church compromised. The Church persisted and handed down to the renewed civilization of the Middle Ages the ideal of a united Christendom. It is only too evident that the ideal was far from being fulfilled by the warring medieval kings and barons. Yet, at the back of men's minds, there was the notion that mankind should form some sort of political unity. You have only to read Dante's *De Monarchia* to meet one version of the contention that, as there was one Church and one pope, so there ought to be one emperor to whom lesser kings owed a measure of allegiance.

The influence of the idea of Christendom, although painfully incomplete in the political sphere, was yet real, and is more evident elsewhere. The universities, with their common Latin language and their scholars drawn from all countries to hear the most famous teachers, were thoroughly international. The Church, too, was international, at a period when Anselm from Aosta could cross the Alps and the Channel to become archbishop of Canterbury, and John of Salisbury could travel in the opposite direction to become bishop of Chartres.

The idea of a united Christendom was finally destroyed, not merely by the weakness of the empire and its conflicts with the papacy, but by the rise of national monarchies. In the fourteenth century Marsilius of Padua is the literary herald of the centralized State, which, as long as it retains the strength, will brook no interference with its affairs from outside. Such are the States to which we are now accustomed, and which have provoked conflicts making the wars of the Middle Ages look like friendly bouts with the gloves.

At the present stage of human history no thoughtful person

can overlook the need of supranational authority. The question is, not only how to bring a sufficient number of men to see this, but how to make them really want it. The intellectual and emotional background of the ideal is missing. There can hardly be a satisfactory answer except from the sense of human solidarity which proceeds from the Christian faith and from membership of the universal Church. This is the sense which, in the midst of what was perhaps the most violent outburst of national exclusiveness in human history, made many of the German clergy risk their lives to provide their interned Polish and other colleagues with the wherewithal to offer the holy Sacrifice, and made the octogenarian cardinal archbishop of Breslau oppose an absolute refusal to the demand of the Nazi authorities that German priests should cease to minister to the Poles whose own pastors had been taken from them. It is in manifestations of this kind, humble though they may appear, rather than in the intricate manoeuvres of international conferences that we may see some real hope of a revived Christendom and a less shattered world.

CHURCH AND STATE

The mention of the Middle Ages brings to mind the general question of the relationship of Church and State which was so much debated and fought out at that period. In our own country, in modern times, we see two solutions of this problem. There is, first of all, the establishment of a Church under the control of the State, with its organization laid down by Act of parliament. But the monopoly rights originally bestowed upon this body by the Acts of Uniformity were eventually withdrawn, and independent religious bodies were and continue to be permitted as private corporations within the State. Although the latter solution is tolerable in practice, neither corresponds with the traditional Christian conception of the relationship of Church and State.

On this view the Church is neither a creation of the State

nor a private body permitted by the State, but an institution independent of any human power and endowed by God himself through Christ with authority in the spiritual sphere. Christ told St Peter and the other apostles that, as the Father had sent him, so also he sent them, and gave them a power of binding and loosing on earth which would be ratified in heaven. Hence the Church asserts a divine right to teach and to legislate in the spiritual order. The Church can ideally demand in all cases, and, where the State consists of men who are her members, can demand practically, that the State should not merely grant her due liberty but should acknowledge her inherent right to all that is required for the fulfilment of her divine mission.

Even a State which does not predominantly consist of sons of the Church can be expected to recognize the distinction of the temporal from the spiritual order. While the State exercises a general superintendence over the terrestrial welfare of man, the Church makes him a citizen of the City of God and provides for his eternal good. The sphere of the Church is distinct from that of the State, and is, in fact, a superior order. In the opinion of some over-enthusiastic medieval canonists, this entailed that the authority of the Church extended in principle to all matters, and that temporal rulers should consider themselves as vassals of the pope. It was only in order to avoid overmuch distraction with temporal business that the Church allowed secular rulers to take over the ordinary business of civil administration.

This is evidently erroneous. The superiority of the spiritual to the temporal does not involve the inclusion of the latter within the former. Neither of these spheres is a part of the other. Although they are organically related, they remain distinct and essentially independent. Both Church and State have full authority in their own spheres, and it is rather a matter for negotiation when a question arises which concerns them in common. But it is still important to observe that, since the spiritual order is autonomous, the Church exists in her own right and not by sufferance of the State. Even less has the State any right to determine the form of ecclesiastical organization.

We can now ask more specifically what the spiritual authority of the Church can vindicate as her own. She claims, of course, full freedom of worship and full freedom of teaching. Christians should be able to receive a Christian education. But, since education is an organic whole, religious teaching cannot be separated from secular teaching without harm to both and to education as a whole. Hence the Church asserts a right to maintain schools and universities. Laws by which a government monopolizes the field of education and forbids the Church and her religious Orders to teach are, consequently, unjust and cannot be recognized by the Church. Where the State gives financial support to popular education, it is only fair that ecclesiastical institutions should receive their proper share of that support.

The Church claims to be unfettered in holding the property required for her purposes and in making the appointments of her bishops and other officials. She claims that her legislation in spiritual matters should be acknowledged as binding upon her subjects. In particular, since marriage is a sacrament of the New Law, the Church asserts an exclusive right to legislate about the marriages of Christians and to judge their validity in particular cases. The authority of her courts is not derived from the State, but should simply be recognized by the State.

Where it is necessary, the Church should be able to call upon the coercive power of the State to implement her decisions. For example, if an ecclesiastical court declared that a marriage is invalid or that a cleric should be deprived of his benefice, the power of the State can rightly be invoked to carry these decisions into effect. In the Middle Ages, when Europe was gradually rising again from the anarchy which followed the collapse of the Roman empire, the ecclesiastical authorities frequently possessed their own means of coercion. The later reaction, typically expressed by Marsilius of Padua, denied to the Church any right of exercising coercion. It would, in fact, be inconvenient in a fully ordered State that the Church should possess the equivalent of an independent police force, and it is rather more consonant with the nature of the Church that she should not do so. It should, nevertheless, be admitted that the Church has the right to ask the State to enforce those of her decisions which require physical enforcement, or the power to make them would be vain.

The full independence and authority of the Church in the spiritual order make it appropriate that the head of the Church should enjoy sovereign temporal independence. The Papal States grew up more or less by accident. When the Western Roman empire was overthrown, there was no one to whom the inhabitants of Rome and the surrounding district could look for protection except the bishop of the once imperial city. The temporal authority of the pope was gradually stabilized and extended, and it was then realized that this afforded a useful guarantee of the independence of the Church. Although it was eventually extended too widely and, as is notorious, engrossed too much of the attention of the Renaissance pontiffs, the principle of the temporal power was so evidently salutary that it could scarcely be given up, even when the movement for the unification of Italy arose in the nineteenth century. Hence Pius IX and his successors refused to acknowledge the right of the Italian government to the territory which had been occupied by force when the troops of the new Italian kingdom breached the walls of Rome by the Porta Pia in 1870. A reasonable solution was reached by the Lateran Treaty of 1929, according to which the pope enjoys full sovereign rights, but over a territory so small that it does no harm to the unity of Italy and could not possibly distract the rulers of the Church from their proper task.

The Church, as the supreme authority in Christian morals, has a certain power of moral judgement over States and governments. While churchmen can rightly be condemned if they attempt to dogmatize on purely political issues, Christian priests and bishops cannot be expected to remain silent when a moral question is involved. Prudence sometimes compels them to keep silence when more harm than good would be done by their intervention, but their right to speak on moral questions is in principle clear. It was on this principle that the medieval popes could in the last resort declare that a ruler had forfeited the allegiance of his subjects. The modern world will not listen to the Church in the same way, but the usual attitude of modern people is deplorably inconsistent. They call loudly upon the Church to preach what they preach and to condemn what they condemn, but, when something is said with which they disagree, they reproach the Church for mixing in politics. If a power of moral judgement be accorded to the Church, this must be independent of contemporary fashions.

Such is the traditional Christian doctrine of the relationship of Church and State, based on the distinction between the spiritual and the temporal order and their mutual independence in their proper concerns. The history of the Middle Ages shows us this doctrine being worked out and established in the concrete, through the action of courageous bishops, like St Anselm and St Thomas of Canterbury, and courageous popes, like St Gregory VII and Innocent III. But it is not merely a piece of medieval history, for it is a permanent exigence of the Church of Christ. It is only the logical enucleation of the authority conferred upon her by her Founder when he said: "All power is given to me in heaven and in earth", and: "As the Father hath sent me, I also send you."

In modern times the liberty of the Church has been greatly curtailed in many countries, and the Church is willing to accept in practice any arrangement which respects her most essential rights. Arrangements with particular States are made by those treaties between the State and the Holy See which are called concordats. An unprejudiced person, looking at the world as it is at present, can hardly venture to assert that the world has gained by pushing the Church into the background. Nevertheless, wherever the Church exists, she continues, by receiving the allegiance of her members in matters of faith and morals, to be a safeguard against the worship of the State and an impassable obstacle to totalitarianism.

CHRISTIANITY AND DEMOCRACY

Finally, we may ask how Christianity stands to that liberal democracy which represents the political outlook of the majority of people in Great Britain and the United States. There is one possible difficulty which is due simply to a confusion of thought. The Christian, acknowledging a divine authority in the Church, is sometimes inclined to cultivate authoritarian notions in politics. The democrat, starting from political individualism, is sometimes inclined to favour a religious individualism which is incompatible with Christian tradition.

It is evident that each is indulging in a formally similar, although materially contrary, confusion of thought. The existence of a divine right in the Church is no reason for attributing absolute authority to governments, nor is the absence of a divine right of governments a reason for denying such a right to the Church in her own province. Each order, the spiritual and temporal, has its own principles, and each question must be considered on its merits. The more analytic thinking of the Middle Ages, indeed, was very insistent on this contrast between the divine authority of the Church and the human contrivance of the secular State. If, in modern times, Christians have often tended unreservedly to support the established order, even when it badly needed reform, the simple explanation is that the forces of change have so frequently been anti-Christian, and the remedy was worse than the disease. The character of the Christian Church is, therefore, no obstacle to political democracy.

In reality we find that liberal democracy has a great deal

in common with Christianity. Both are fundamentally engaged with the dignity of the human person and the brotherhood of man. Liberal democracy is still living upon ideas derived from the Christian Middle Ages and the political philosophy of St Thomas Aquinas. If you want to see whence the central ideas of writers like Locke and Mill are ultimately derived, you will find them in the section on law in the *Prima Secundae* of the *Summa Theologica*.

But you will find them there with a difference. Where the name of God has disappeared from the pages of Mill, and occupies a relatively minor place in Locke, St Thomas anchors all human law upon the eternal divine law and all human sovereignty upon the sovereignty of God. It would be foolish to pretend that this makes no difference. Whether God exists is not a departmental question; your decision here is a pervasive fact, subtly altering everything else in your outlook.

On the whole, the modern liberal democrat tries to treat the existence of God as if it were a departmental question. If he is a conscientious agnostic, he can scarcely do anything else. But, even if he is a theist and a Christian in some sense, although not perhaps quite in the sense in which the term has been here understood, his religion usually remains outside his politics. He thinks religion a good thing, especially for children, and even for adults if they are not called upon to believe or do anything in particular, but this religion is hardly more than a decorous background or an occasional means of emotional uplift. The notion that God and the Church must come first, or can make absolute demands upon him, is very far from his mind, and he is prepared cheerfully to sacrifice the interests of religion for the sake of what he regards as social reform.

The Christian, on the other hand, if he is genuinely a Christian, cannot do other than place God first and relate his other beliefs and activities to his religion. He could not be satisfied with his political philosophy unless he thought that it approximated to the truth eternally contemplated by the divine mind. He reverences every individual human soul especially because it is made for the beatific vision of God, and he believes in the brotherhood of man especially because he holds that God has called all men into his Church. Human affairs are sadly mixed, and, when there is only a choice between two partial goods, he feels bound to prefer a government which allows due liberty to Christian practice to one which, while in other respects coming nearer to his political ideal, yet threatens to be anti-Christian.

Human affairs are, at present, still more sadly mixed than usual, and there is much to bring together the Christian and the liberal humanitarian, even if only in opposition to tendencies which both abhor. They have, indeed, enough positively in common for a great deal of fruitful collaboration. Yet it is intellectually contemptible to gloss over differences when they really exist. While the Christian and the liberal humanitarian can agree about the second commandment of the new law and the love of one's neighbour, the Christian will always shock his associate by insisting that the greatest and the first commandment is this: "Thou shalt love the Lord thy God with thy whole heart and with thy whole soul and with thy whole mind."

The Christian, therefore, cannot compete with the progressive secularist, and it would be foolish of him to attempt to do so, talking of the Christian revolution and so forth. While the progressive secularist, with his pathetic hopefulness, beckons to a beautiful world which awaits men round the corner if they will only do one or two eminently reasonable things, the Christian knows that the world will always be full of misery and evil, and that there will always be a contrast between the city of this world and the city of God. While the progressive secularist can devote his whole energies to social reform and sacrifice himself nobly for the cause, the Christian will prosaically invite him to the apparently selfish achievement of supernatural life in union with God. Hence the Christian will be condemned as cynical and indifferent to human ills, even though a few old-fashioned and overcrowded convents of nuns can astonishingly do more for the happiness of the poor, the sick and the orphan than all the most expensive governmental schemes.

For the Christian remembers that, while Martha was anxious and troubled about many things, there was one thing necessary. The advice to seek first the kingdom of God, and all these things will be added unto you, is familiar enough, but it is worth noticing, first, that it is a strange paradox and, secondly, that it is of considerable moment. For, in relation to our subject, it means that, if politics and social reform are put in the first place, they will inevitably become distorted and exaggerated, and that the only way to establish a sound political and social order is to put these aims in the second place and to pursue primarily something else. But is it not perhaps true that the political ills of our own day are largely due to politics having received an exaggerated importance? This may be a damping conclusion, but, on Christian principles, it suggests itself rather forcibly.

EPILOGUE

The following passages from the Gospels will be readily seen to sum up the central emphasis of Christ's moral teaching.

"Unless your justice abound more than that of the scribes and pharisees, you shall not enter into the kingdom of heaven" (Matt. 5. 20).

"When you shall have done all these things that are commanded you, say: We are unprofitable servants; we have done that which we ought to do" (Luke 17. 10).

"You have heard that it hath been said: Thou shalt love thy neighbour and hate thy enemy. But I say to you: Love your enemies; do good to them that hate you; and pray for them that persecute and calumniate you ... For if you love them that love you, what reward shall you have? Do not even the publicans this? And if you salute your brethren only, what do you more? Do not also the heathens this? Be you therefore perfect, as also your heavenly Father is perfect" (Matt. 5. 43–4, 46–8).

"Thou shalt love the Lord thy God with thy whole heart and with thy whole soul and with thy whole mind and with thy whole strength. This is the first commandment. And the second is like to it: Thou shalt love thy neighbour as thyself" (Mark 12. 30–31).

SELECT BIBLIOGRAPHY

In this series:

BARS, Henry: *Faith, Hope and Charity*; DAUJAT, Jean: *The Theology of Grace*; LIÉGÉ, P.-A., O.P.: *What is Christian Life?*; TREVETT, Reginald F.: *Sex and the Christian* (American edn, *The Church and Sex*).

Among the few Catholic general treatments of Christian ethics in English may be mentioned:

D'ARCY, M. C., S.J.: *Christian Morals*, London and New York, Longmans, 1937; *The Mind and Heart of Love*, London, Faber, and New York, Holt, 1945; *The Meeting of Love and Knowledge*, London, Allen and Unwin, and New York, Harper, 1958.

GILLMAN, Gerard, S.J.: *The Primacy of Charity in Moral Theology*, London, Burns and Oates, and Westminster, Md, Newman Press, 1960.

PIEPER, J.: *Justice*, London, Faber, 1957, and New York, Pantheon, 1955.

VANN, G., O.P.: *Morals Makyth Man*, London and New York, Longmans, 1938.

Among other Christian contemporary approaches in English:

BRUNNER, E.: *The Divine Imperative*, Philadelphia, Westminster Press, 1943.

GORE, C.: *The Philosophy of the Good Life*, in the Everyman series, London, Dent, New York, Dutton (n.d.).

LEWIS, C. S.: *The Four Loves*, London, Bles, and New York, Macmillan, 1960.

ROBINSON, N. H. G.: *Christ and Conscience*, Welwyn, Nisbet, 1956.

The Twentieth Century Encyclopedia of Catholicism

The number of each volume indicates its place in the over-all series and not the order of publication.

TWENTIETH CENTURY ENCYCLOPEDIA OF CATHOLICISM

All titles are subject to change.